The Furniture Machine
Furniture since 1990

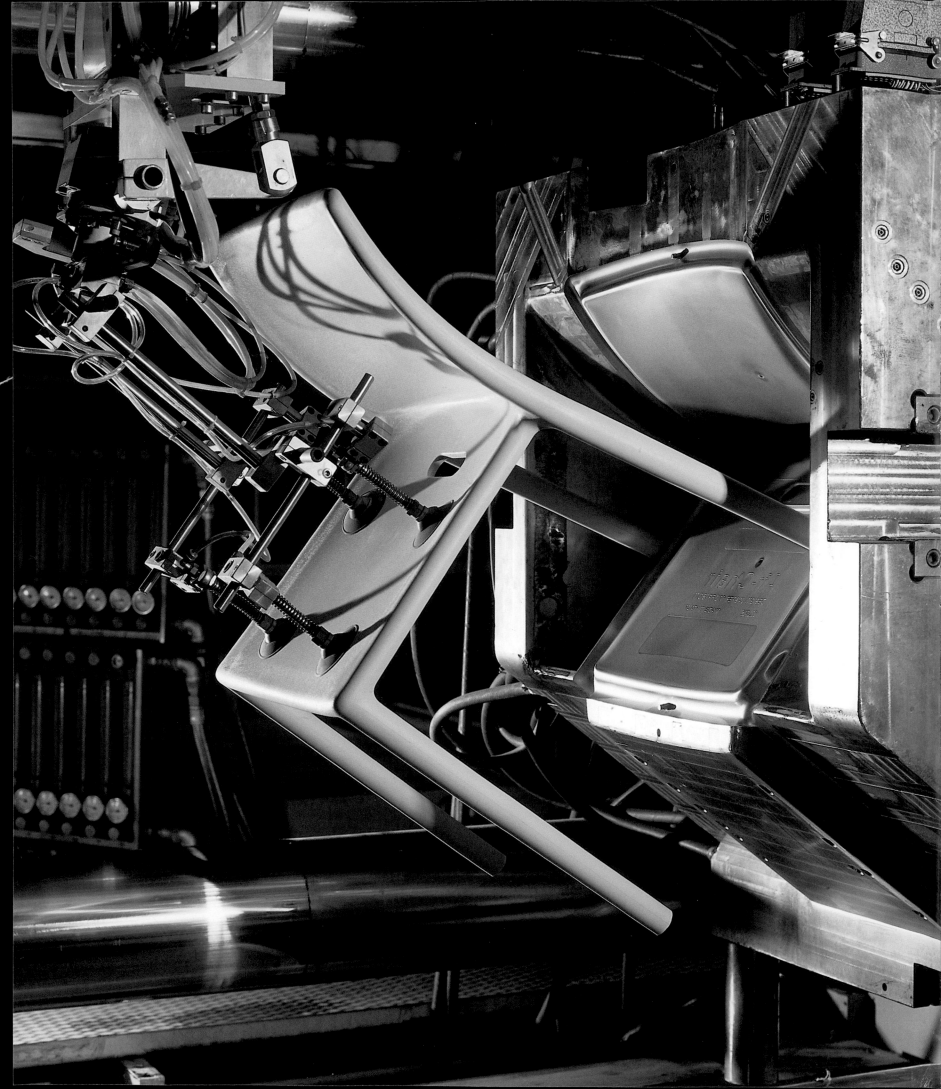

The Furniture Machine
Furniture since 1990

Gareth Williams

V&A Publications

First published by V&A Publications, 2006
V&A Publications
Victoria and Albert Museum
South Kensington
London SW7 2RL

Distributed in North America by Harry N.
Abrams, Inc., New York

Hardback edition
ISBN-10 1851774947
ISBN-13 9781851774944
Library of Congress Control Number
2006928680
10 9 8 7 6 5 4 3 2 1
2010 2009 2008 2007 2006

A catalogue record for this book is available
from the British Library.

Every effort has been made to seek permission
to reproduce those images whose copyright
does not reside with the V&A, and we are
grateful to the individuals and institutions
who have assisted in this task. Any omissions
are entirely unintentional, and the details
should be addressed to V&A Publications.

Publication & Typefaces designed
by A2/SW/HK
New V&A Photography by Mike Kitcatt,
V&A Photographic Studio

Jacket illustration: Cinderella table,
designed by Jeroen Verhoeven, edition
of 20 self-production, the Nederlands,
2005, CNC-cut plywood. V&A:W.1-2006

Frontispiece: Air chair, design by Jasper
Morrison, coming out of the mould,
manufactured by Magis, Italy 1999.
Photo: Ramak Fazel/Domus.

Printed in China

V&A Publications
Victoria and Albert Museum
South Kensington
London SW7 2RL
www.vam.ac.uk

Contents

Introduction

The Changing Landscape of Furniture

'I mainly work for industries. I cannot judge my work but I always try to bridge human need and companies' conveniences, ecological consciousness and business, philosophy and market research, progress and investment limitations, art and functionality, beauty and comfort, freedom of choice and production limitations, experimentation and concreteness, sensuality and technology, optimism and economic crisis, education and consumerism, happiness and a stressful life, contemplation and speed, intimacy and status, domesticity and public relations...' [1]

Michele de Lucchi

A designer, it seems, must be all things to all people, and he or she must learn to balance conflicting demands. But De Lucchi also makes clear that design does not take place in isolation, in the designer's studio, but is an active process involving manufacturers and the market. *The Furniture Machine* explores this process and some of the constraints and contradictions it presents. It maps the world of contemporary furniture, revealing the network of designers and manufacturers who dominate it, and how design is mediated and represented to its growing audience and customer base. This network, though extensive, is not worldwide but is focused on Europe and parts of Asia and North America, and the content of the book reflects this. In this Introduction I shall examine the context for furniture design today; the education system that produces designers; the regional and national variations that influence furniture design; and the scope of the manufacturing industry and the mechanism of trade shows.

This book is not about *all* furniture that is designed and made, but about what Dr Judy Attfield, Leverhulme Emeritus Research Fellow in Design History at Southampton University, calls 'things with attitude': consciously design-heavy, highly visible and charged objects that stand out against the sea

of 'everyday things' that are made and used. [2] These are the objects and furniture that lead changes in taste and contribute to defining the visual and material culture of the age. As such, inevitably they are made for a very small elite who can afford to own them, and by no means represent the belongings of the vast majority of people, or the appearance of their homes. Even low-cost high-design, such as moulded plastic chairs, are expensive, relative to the cost of most furniture. Yet contemporary furniture – and by correlation, contemporary interior design and architecture, with music, art and particularly fashion – is part of a seductive lifestyle industry that is marketed at us by the media. We may aspire to own this furniture, and we know about it from magazines and makeover shows, even if we lack sufficient wealth to own it. We can buy *into* it, even if we cannot buy it.

Nor is this book about academic critical discourse concerning design. Instead, it seeks to look at the ways in which furniture is designed, mediated and consumed in the real world, albeit a relatively exclusive, high-end and design-conscious world. This explains the inclusion here of the designers' own words about their work, as well as my use of design journalism as a barometer of changing trends and attitudes through the period.

Casablanca sideboard, designed
by Ettore Sottsass, manufactured
by Memphis, Italy, 1981. Plastic
laminate over fibreboard. V&A:
W.14-1990, purchased with the
assistance of the manufacturer.

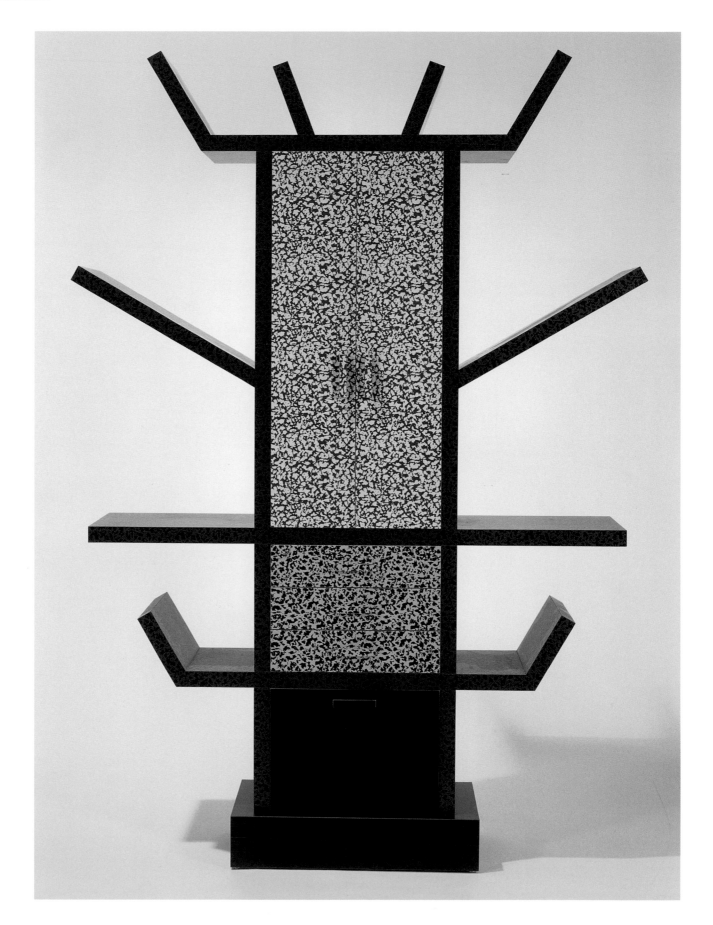

Prototype Wait chairs, designed by Matthew Hilton, UK, 1996–8, CNC-cut wood example made by Matthew Hilton. Injection-moulded polypropylene example made by Authentics, Germany. V&A: W.17&18-2005, given by Matthew Hilton.

Computer-generated stress tests for the Air chair, designed by Jasper Morrison for Magis, Italy, 1997–9. Courtesy of Magis.

Droog Design exhibition, Milan, 1993, including chair designed by Gijs Bakker, 1989, and Milk Bottle lamp, designed by Tejo Remy, 1991. Photo: courtesy of Droog Design.

There are several landmarks in the history of late twentieth-century furniture. One is the exhibition 'Italy, the New Domestic Landscape' held at the Museum of Modern Art in New York in 1972, which suggested the title for this introductory chapter.[3] It charted the rise of experimental Italian design during the 1960s and marked the watershed at which mid-century modernism, hitherto dominated by American and Scandinavian designers, gave way to a far more conceptual and radical modernism from Italy. Italian predominance in the design of furniture was reiterated by another landmark: the arrival in 1981 of Memphis, the Milan-based collective of young furniture and product designers, led by Ettore Sottsass, that went on to dominate design in the 1980s. With a few collections and a lot of hullabaloo, Memphis reintroduced decoration, kitsch, postmodernism and low taste as high culture. Memphis furniture truly was 'things with attitude'. With prescience, Deyan Sudjic, founding editor of *Blueprint*, recognized its significance. 'The real lessons of the Memphis movement, however, will be the double-edged nature of media attention, and the way design is trivialized when turned into fodder for the consumption of an image-obsessed society. And that is a challenging issue for all design, whatever its stylistic vocabulary.'[4]

If the 1980s were dominated by Memphis, what were the landmarks that followed? Arguably the most significant and immediate was the launch of Droog Design in 1993, which refocused ideas about the purpose and expression of design away

from the polished symbolic gestures of the Italians towards the domestically scaled, ironic and provisional objects of the Dutch. Droog Design certainly knew how to manipulate the media-driven, image-based society described by Sudjic. However, before Droog Design, in the mid- and late 1980s, a spirit of minimalism and functionalism re-entered design, typified by Jasper Morrison's work, but not confined to him. Morrison also represents a renaissance in British design, particularly the reputation of British-born or-based furniture designers on the world (read: Italian) stage. By the mid-1990s European manufacturers wielding international clout were clamouring for British designers.

On the broader world stage, concerns about sustainable design entered the mainstream as a by-product of environmental consciousness, and engendered responses from furniture designers. Geo-political issues also shaped the period. Western societies became increasingly anxious about their status and security in the light of fundamentalism and terrorism on one hand, and on the other dynamic economic expansion in the East. These anxieties realized themselves as cautiousness by manufacturers, but also yielded interesting responses from designers.

Undoubtedly a major landmark in the landscape of furniture was the international expansion of the Swedish firm IKEA. In Britain the period from the early 1950s to about 1980 had been symbolized by the Scandinavian-inspired furniture of G-Plan, but when IKEA reached Britain in 1987, it shook the furniture manufacturing and retailing industries by radically transforming how the majority consumed furniture.[5] Most importantly in the context of this book, it put 'things with attitude' within reach of general consumers, not just economically, but psychologically and geographically too. In 1993 G-Plan went into receivership; another minor landmark in the changing landscape of furniture.

The design process has been transformed since 1990 as computer-aided design and manufacturing (CAD-CAM) has taken hold. In 1990 designers still made traditional models of their furniture to test ergonomics and to refine appearances. Increasingly model-making by hand has given way to virtual modelling on screen and the production of models and prototypes using techniques such as laser sintering. Computers have even affected the shape of furniture as compound curves for mouldings and complex structures are much easier to achieve this way. However, the point of making models and prototypes still remains: to test a design against numerous criteria, including structural, aesthetic and cost demands, and thereby guard against commercial failure of the finished product as much as possible. Only the means have changed. When Italian plastics specialists Magis developed Jasper Morrison's Air chair (1997–9), for example, the design was tested on screen, virtually, to calculate areas of stress and to work out minute details, such as the optimum angle for the injection tool. Previously models would have been constructed. CAD-CAM effectively speeds up the design process and production too, as digitized designs can be emailed to factories anywhere in the world instantaneously. Ron Arad tells the story of designing a modular bottle rack for leading Italian manufacturer Kartell that existed only on screen: he did not see a model or prototype, or any three-dimensional version of his design until he saw the product displayed in the showroom window.

Other landmarks of the period include the 1989 founding of both the Design Museum in London and the Vitra Design Museum in Weil-am-Rhein, designed by Frank Gehry. Both museums signalled the emergence of a new level of appreciation of twentieth-century and contemporary design. At the opening of the Vitra Design Museum Rolf Fehlbaum, Vitra's chairman and son of its founder, said: 'Good design is not like art. But it is as good as art. It is autonomous; it is neither applied art, nor is it small architecture.'[6] This was the period in which furniture design came out from the shadow of architecture, and began to be treated with the same seriousness as art. In many ways Vitra has changed public taste too. Since 1957, when Vitra acquired the licence to manufacture Herman Miller furniture in Europe, it has been at the forefront of design and technology in furniture production, working with Verner Panton, Mario Bellini, Antonio Citterio, Jasper Morrison and Ron Arad, right through to young designers such as Ronan and Erwan Bouroullec. Vitra is primarily an office furniture company, but Fehlbaum is also a collector of furniture and Vitra Editions, begun in 1988, has manufactured many significant designs, primarily seating, by elite designers. Fehlbaum explains: 'The routine production of office furniture leaves little room for experimental design. So we commission a series that does not have to fall in line with an existing product range, nor be fixed by a single design tendency. There are no rules and regulations imposed by market penetration that lead to barriers

Interior of the Vitra Design Museum,
Weil-am-Rhein, Germany, designed
by Frank Gehry, 1989. Photo: Vitra
Design Museum / Peter Inselmann.

Ottagono, 151, June 2002.

against creative experiment.'[7] Effectively, Vitra attempts to remove some of the constraints identified by De Lucchi in order to make 'things with attitude' while not inconsequentially reinforcing its brand image. Vitra has greatly contributed to – and benefited from – the collectors' market that has arisen for contemporary design and also drove the resurgence of interest in mid-century modern design. In the US Herman Miller reissued designs by Charles and Ray Eames from 1994. Vitra, which owns the European rights to the designs, as well as the studio archive, conscientiously and assiduously promoted their back catalogue, fuelling an Eames-mania that crested in about 1998.[8]

The idea of the celebrity designer has taken hold. Celebrity designers are the coterie who are globally famous within the sphere of furniture design, and in the case of someone like Philippe Starck, may also be a household name. The furniture industry, like the fashion

industry and the art market, creates this elite that I shall term here the 'egosystem'. The egosystem, like the concept of the ecosystem that is consciously evoked, exists through a symbiotic process that benefits all parties in the relationship. The media needs new trophies in the form of new designers to celebrate. Manufacturers need designers whose work is recognized and desirable, to add competitiveness and value to their products. Designers themselves aspire to positions of influence and success. For the aspirant public, celebrity designers fulfil the role of taste-makers, even role models, humanizing a faceless industry and adding caché to the top-end products they design. The egosystem can only be a small group at any given time, since to remain elite it must remain exclusive.

The egosystem has also infiltrated design education, not least because major stars like Ron Arad are also leading educators. Judy Attfield argues that 'The current post-industrial climate in Britain has seen a change of attitude in design education, turning away from training designers to serve a rapidly contracting, almost defunct national industrial sector, to treating them more like international fine artists, placing greater emphasis on self-motivation to prepare them for freelance work in the global market.'[9] This inevitably leads to more conceptual and experimental work, high in visual impact and content, but low on practicality or usefulness: 'things with attitude'. They are what the writer and former Design Museum director Alice Rawsthorn calls 'mediagenic' designs: objects that can command a magazine spread or dominate a television studio set. She was writing about Marc Newson, author of myriad 'mediagenic' designs, who also embodies how the designer-as-celebrity becomes part of the media-driven consumption of design.[10] Today, it seems that design graduates need to promote themselves as personalities because it is no longer sufficient to let the work speak for itself.

Furniture design education in the international arena is dominated by a handful of schools. Milan's Domus Academy and the Politecnico di Milano – the city's university for engineering, architecture and industrial design – no longer generate the high-profile graduates they once did, perhaps signalling that Milan's status as pre-eminent design city is now challenged. London's Royal College of Art (RCA) attracts students from around the world, and its staff and graduates – too many to list – now sit at the top tables of the design industry, and design them too! Many appear in these pages, and the network of RCA designers infiltrates the entire contemporary furniture industry, much as a college like Central Saint Martins dominates high fashion. Both colleges helped to make London a vibrant and vital design hub in the 1990s. Design Academy Eindhoven has capitalized on and focused the resurgence of design innovation in the Netherlands.[11] Without doubt it produces talented designers, as does Konstfack (the University College of Arts, Crafts and Design in Stockholm), ECAL (École Cantonale d'Art de Lausanne, Switzerland, headed by the ebullient Pierre Keller) and the art school in Saint Etienne, France (École régionale des Beaux-Arts de Saint-Etienne). In Britain, furniture design is often taught together with product or industrial design. It is given particular prominence at Buckinghamshire Chilterns University College in High Wycombe (which has a long tradition of furniture manufacturing, now sadly almost ended), and at Ravensbourne College of Design and Communication and Kingston University, both on London's outer fringes. The now-defunct private Parnham College, run by the designer-maker John Makepeace in Dorset, produced notable graduates in very different furniture sectors in the form of David Linley, Wales and Wales and Konstantin Grcic.

One aspect of furniture design that has not dramatically changed since 1990 is that it is still dominated by men and by a masculine sensibility aligned with engineering and architecture. Within the 'egosystem' perhaps the only women designers are Patricia Urquoila and Hella Jongerius. There are talented and famous women designers – Tomoko Azumi in London, for example, and Matali Crasset in Paris – and influential women in other aspects of the industry, such as the Italian industrialist Patrizia Moroso, the founder of Droog Design Renny Ramakers, and Lidewij Edelcoort, the head of Design Academy Eindhoven. The development of furniture as part of the lifestyle industry, which is examined in Chapter Six, is interlinked with fashion and interiors, and there has been a rise in the number of women working in this sphere. It remains to be seen whether the number of women furniture designers increases as a result, and how they will change the industry.

Nationality and national identity still play a role in furniture design, despite (or perhaps, because of) an ever-expanding global market, falling trade barriers, and

easier and swifter international communications. It is possible to talk about a specifically Dutch design sensibility that is ironic, cool and ethical, and about content over styling. Swedish design, too, has retained a strong visual identity based on harmonious comfort and accessible modernism, drawing on a rich design heritage, and only latterly has an edgier, more spontaneous *frisson* begun to emerge.[12] Both nations actively promote their designers abroad as cultural exports supported by state agencies. In Italy, still the powerhouse of the international furniture industry, there is little state promotion of design or designers, but very well-organized and powerful trade bodies exist instead. The federation of wood, cork, furniture and furnishing industries, Federlegno-Arredo, keenly promotes Italian furniture abroad, exploiting Italy's reputation for high design, innovation, luxury, craftsmanship and technical excellence. Similar trade bodies exist for ceramics, architectural fittings and the stone industries. Traditionally all these manufacturers only worked with Italian designers, but latterly (as this book shows) they have looked abroad for design talent. Therefore Italian furniture faces an identity crisis as the older generation of *maestri*, who have dominated Italian aesthetics for half a century, die off with few obvious successors at home.

Storm chair, designed and made
by Stephen Richards at Parnham
College, UK, 2000. Various woods
including ash, sycamore, walnut,
oak and elm, jointed and glued
together. V&A: W.1-2003,
given by Stephen Richards.

Milking stool, designed by
Pearson Lloyd, for the exhibition
'Le Botte-cul', organized by the École
Cantonale d'Art de Lausanne (ÉCAL),
Centre Culturel Suisse, Milan, 10-15
April, 2002. Customized watering
can. Photo: Pierre Fantys.

Import Export: Global Influences
in Contemporary Design, exhibition
design by Gitta Gschwendtner,
including furniture by Shin and
Tomoko Azumi, Victoria and Albert
Museum, London 20 September –
4 December 2005. Photo: V&A.

In Britain, however, there is little by way of furniture manufacturing and the pool of design talent, though internationally recognized, also comprises a rich mix of overseas designers. In the twentieth century the unofficial national style was Arts and Crafts, but the craft revival since the 1970s is relatively parochial, contributing little to international design trends. 'Craft' stubbornly remains distant from 'design' in Britain, although in Sweden, Italy and elsewhere the traditions are more integrated. It is not possible, therefore, to talk of a prevailing coherent British national furniture design, though in other disciplines such as fashion and architecture this could be argued for. State support of design is divided between different ministries and bodies that include the Design Council and the British Council, both of which organize exhibitions to tour abroad, and there is no trade body with the influence or understanding of the furniture industry to compare with those in Italy. By exhibiting their work, the British Council

regularly makes 'honorary Brits' of foreign nationals such as Mathias Bengtsson (a Swede) and Tord Boontje (Dutch) because they live, or have lived, in Britain, in recognition of the schizophrenic and multicultural identity of design in Britain today. The exhibition 'Import Export: Global Influences in Contemporary Design', held in 2005, acknowledged this dichotomy; it explored how British design has influenced, and been influenced by, other world cultures, and included work by Tord Boontje, Gitta Gschwendtner and Shin and Tomoko Azumi.[13]

French design is emerging from the long shadow cast by Philippe Starck (born 1949), whose towering presence since the 1980s has tended to dwarf other talented designers. Olivier Mourgue, for example, though only a decade older than Starck, seems to represent a previous generation of designers active in the 1960s and 1970s. If there is an identifiable French style today, it resides dually in the grand tradition of the *décorateur* (embodied by the cool classicism of Andrée Putman) and the optimistic utopianism of radical 1960s design (Mourgue): the influence of both resonates through the work of younger designers. The French government actively supports design both at home and on the international stage. Since 1964 a national collection of contemporary furniture has been formed, principally to furnish the presidential Elysée Palace. It is a collection of modern furniture by leading French designers intentionally formed to signal the modernity of the French State. Nothing like it exists elsewhere. VIA (Valorisation de l'innovation dans l'ameublement), founded in 1979 by the Ministère de l'Industrie, promotes and supports young designers. The promotion of young designers, therefore, is a way national identities are reinforced and projected. Germany, despite being Europe's highest spender on contemporary furniture, surprisingly does not actively promote itself through design, or present its design industry on the world stage. It is still possible to identify a national taste for modernity and engineered precision in the output of companies such as Interlübke, but with the notable exception of lighting guru Ingo Maurer, there is little wit in German design. The United States has signally failed to embrace the type of international furniture design explored in this book, outside the coastal urban centres. The great design heritage of the mid-twentieth century is entirely overlooked at home, in complete contrast to the veneration American designers Charles and Ray Eames, Harry Bertoia, Eero Saarinen

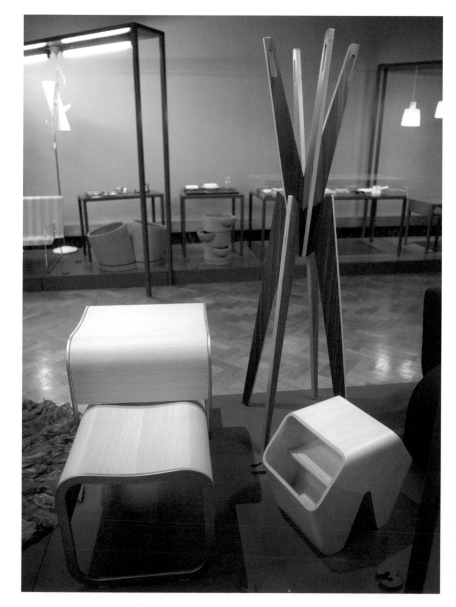

Fiera Milano exhibition complex
at Rho-Pero, Milan, designed
by Massimiliano Fuksas, 2001-5.
Photo: courtesy of fieramilano.

Neues Messegelände

Salone Internazionale
del Mobile und
Internationale
Einrichtungszubehörmesse:
■ Klassisch / Ethnisch / Fusion
■ Design
■ Modern

☐ Eurocucina, International
Küchenmöbelmesse
■ Eimu, International
Büromöbelmesse
■ Internationale
Bad-Ambiente-Messe
☐ FTK *Technology*
For the Kitchen
☐ SaloneSatellite

■ M1 rote Linie
■ Parkplätze
◉ Eingänge
◯ Kongress- und
Dienstleistungszentrum:
Pressebüro /
Ausstellersekretariat

and the rest receive in Europe. American designers, such as Jeffrey Bernett and Stephen Burks, look to Europe for inspiration and for manufacturers, but the bulk of work by young designers appears naïve and directionless when compared to European equivalents.

The enormity of the global furniture trade cannot be underestimated since it furnishes the homes, schools, workplaces and other buildings visited daily by many of the six and half billion people alive today.[14] The engines of the industry are the trade shows, cheerless and exhausting events caricatured by the designer and architect Dinah Casson as 'too many products in too small a space with not enough to say, being propped up by too many salesmen in too small a space with too much to say.'[15] A staggering 326 trade shows in 63 countries were scheduled for 2005 devoted to the wood, furniture and furnishings sector, kicking off with the West African International Trade Expo in Lagos, Nigeria (12-14 January) and rounding up on Christmas Day at the Mebeles International Furniture Exhibition in Riga, Latvia (22-25 December). Most fairs are in Europe, in 30 nations from Ireland to Russia. The furniture trade does not target Central Africa at all, but exhibitions such as KazBuild (7-10 September 2005 in Almaty, Kazakhstan) demonstrate its reach. A growing number of exhibitions across the Russian Federation and China is evidence of increased global trade in these previously closed markets.[16] Only a tiny proportion of the furniture trade is engaged with contemporary design. Even at the prestigious exhibitions, such as the Milan Salone del Mobile, 'Design', 'Modern' and 'Classic' furniture styles are exhibited separately.

In Europe, Italian manufacturers determine the operations of the furniture industry, even though Italian designers are showing signs of waning influence. No other nation's furniture industry can compete in size or ambition, or contribute so much to national coffers and sense of identity. The unique composition of the Italian furniture industry is its strength and also defines its character. Small and medium-sized firms, often family owned and run, form an intricate network of services and specialisms. These can be very highly technical: for example, the casting and shaping of metal components, or the moulding of plastics. Small firms, though independent, form intimate relationships with each other with the effect that in several areas, such as the region around Udine in the north-east, groups of companies working together form their own infrastructure. Because they are small, these firms can be flexible and responsive to the market. Because they are specialized, they have developed levels of expertise and artisanship that cannot be found elsewhere. Many critics have observed that Italian furniture manufacturing falls somewhere between craft and industry, requiring equal measures of technological investment and manual skill. This means relatively small production runs of experimental techniques, or innovative products, are possible. The Italian industry, therefore, does not rely on a few behemoths mass-producing a handful of tried and tested products very cheaply for a bottom-end market. Rather, its strength lies in the diversity of products, backed up by levels of investment in design, research and technical development unmatched elsewhere, manufactured by a vast raft of companies.

The 2,200 companies affiliated to Federlegno-Arredo, the Italian trade organization for furniture manufacturers, generate sales of 40 billion euros annually, of which a third is exported.[17] The federation's subsidiary company, Cosmit (Comitato Organizzatore del Salone del Mobile Italiano), organizes the annual Salone del Mobile in Milan each April, the largest of all the furniture trade shows. Many of the most established Italian manufacturers, including Molteni, Cassina and Moroso, expanded from craft workshops or were founded in the immediate aftermath of World War II, and their output contributed to the post-war reconstruction of the nation. By the late 1950s domestic trade was static but exports were negligible too. A body called Italian Furniture Impex (Ifi) was formed in 1958 to develop promotional opportunities for furniture, in response to a widespread concern for the future of the Italian furniture industry. Inspired by the joint exhibition by Nordic countries in 1960 at the Cologne Möbelmesse (the leading trade fair at the time), Ifi convened a co-operative Italian event at the Cologne fair in 1961 on the grounds that 'If the Scandinavians have succeeded in imposing their style on the world, why shouldn't we be successful in imposing ours?'[18] The first Milan Salone grew out of Ifi and was staged in September that year. It certainly succeeded in imposing Italian style in the intervening four and a half decades, partly by excluding overseas exhibitors altogether until 1967, and then by limiting them to biennial exhibitions until 1991.[19] This enabled the Italian manufacturers to establish themselves domestically and also to create a huge export market. By 2004 the number of exhibitors had swollen six-fold to over 1,900, and visitor numbers

had spiralled to 190,000, a 15-fold increase in comparison to the first Salone in 1961. As an indicator of the increasing internationalism of the event, for the first time there were more overseas visitors than there were Italians.

The Cologne Furniture Fair (Internationale Möbelmesse, or IMM) was founded in 1949 as part of the city's post-war reconstruction effort, and is the other major European furniture trade show. In Milan, the fair is organized by the furniture industry itself; in Cologne it is done by the owners of the site (Koelnmesse GmbH). Both fairs are enormous, though in terms of visitors and exhibitors, Milan steals a march.[20] In 2006 the Salone del Mobile moved to a new fairground on the city fringe, designed by Massimiliano Fuksas, but it is too soon to gauge the effect of the move on the character of the fair.

The other international fairs that lay emphasis on contemporary design are all younger than Milan and Cologne, and their founding is an indicator of the increasing maturity of the contemporary furniture market, reflected in the quality and diversity of products on offer. Trade fairs both respond and contribute to the formation of markets. Ian Rudge and Rachel Robin were fair organizers, not designers or manufacturers. Their decision to found 100% Design in London in 1994 was made in part because they observed a niche in the market that was not being served by other fairs. Rudge recalled: 'We … knew that the anti-Thatcherite punk generation were of an age where they were going to have to buy furniture and there was no way that they were going to be buying the same products as their parents or Thatcher's "Barrett Home" generation.'[21]

Rudge and Robin's 100% Design rapidly became the locus for a period of renewed vigour in British design that was especially associated with young designers, many of whom appear on these pages. Some, such as Inflate and Michael Young, first exhibited at 100% Design. The fair had aspirations to be international from the outset, and through a process of jury selection for the exhibitors (which is not usual for a trade fair) this show has remained small yet elite, balancing big international brands with first-time exhibitors supported by bursaries. Fairs emphasizing contemporary furniture design take place elsewhere, for example in New York (International Contemporary Furniture Fair, or ICFF), Stockholm, Belgium (Kortrijk), Paris, Valencia, Udine and Verona (Arbitare il Tempo). None of these fairs is more than a fraction of the size of Milan or Cologne and

100% Design, London. Exhibition design by Tim Pyne, 22–25 September 2005. Photo: Philip Vile.

all attract considerably smaller audiences.[22] An interesting recent development has been the internationalization of trade shows that are firmly associated with their home cities: 100% Design Moscow was followed by 100% Design Tokyo, while Cosmit launched a Salone in New York and announced plans for a London fair.

The proliferation of trade shows has encouraged the growth of fringe events that, in a sense, convert them from closed business-to-business events into public, cultural occasions. In Milan, all types of furniture, even radical and experimental design, were presented within the confines of the Salone until the 1980s. During that decade major manufacturers, normally the backbone of trade shows, began a drift towards presenting new collections in their permanent showrooms rather than taking stands within the Salone. At the same time non-Italian companies, blocked from exhibiting in the Salone, created an unofficial fringe programme in a variety of venues around Milan, in a bid to get their work seen too. During the 1990s the fringe expanded rapidly until more than 200 exhibitions would be staged across the city to coincide with the main event. Many of these shows are by the young or the disaffected, and are closer to art installations than to product launches. Ron Arad, for example, only exhibited once at the Salone (his stand was swamped with curious visitors), but ever since he has occupied various 'off-site' galleries. Design magazines such as *Interni* publish guides to the events and give them a unified identity. Crucially, the fringe is open to all, not just trade visitors, and the Salone itself began to look like the maiden aunt of wild and exciting offspring. The organizers countered this trend in two ways. From 1997 they gave over one pavilion of the fairground to some 180 young designers selected by jury each year, in an attempt to attract young talent and some excitement back into the show. They named it SalonSatellite, with the suggestion that it was an 'official fringe' event, and even ticketed access separately to the main part of the fair. Its aim was to connect manufacturers with new design talent from Italy and elsewhere. Secondly, a programme of installations and cultural exhibitions, associated with the furniture fair and its sister fairs for kitchens and lighting, were staged in public spaces in the city. These, it was hoped, would take the Salone out of the fairground and capture some of the raw energy conducted by the fringe events. The fringe and the Salone now exist in mutual dependency, one a free-market,

mixed bag of new designers and established names, the other a highly organized, integrated market-place. In Cologne the fringe events are unified under the Passagen banner, and StylePark, a design promotion organization based in Frankfurt, plans group exhibitions on the fringes of all the major furniture fairs.

In London, 100% Design inspired fringe events in 1998 in the form of Designers Block, organized by Piers Roberts and Rory Dodd, co-owners of Same, one of the city's short-lived emporia for leading-edge design in the 1990s. In Roberts' view, 'We just create an open platform to allow people to present their ideas. We don't have a philosophy or an aesthetic.'[23] He is right on the first point, but a criticism levelled at Designers Block was that it presented international young designers without particular attention to their quality, a case of 'Designers Block seeming to suffer from designer's block', as one magazine put it.[24] The exhibition has had a clear aesthetic, however, deriving from the semi-derelict venues that included, most dramatically, the Midland Hotel in St Pancras. The dereliction and provisional quality of the spaces created the right kind of 'avant-gardist' atmosphere, as if visitors were discovering an artist in his garret. Its advantage to exhibitors was the cheapness and availability of space compared to showing at 100% Design itself, and as has already been observed about Milan, some designers associate more with an edgy fringe than with a staid trade fair. Fringe events, therefore, give depth and variety to the furniture trade circuit. Since 1998 100% Design sponsored 100% Guaranteed, a guide to fringe events in London, effectively taking ownership of it by providing unified information, maps to venues, and even free transport. In 2005 100% East was launched in London's Brick Lane, firmly in the territory occupied by fringe exhibitions. It was specifically intended to showcase graduate designers, and in a sense was an 'official' fringe event. For its part Designers Block has developed overseas exhibitions of British talent in Tokyo, New York and Seoul, but faces competitive new arrivals on the London fringe such as the curator and writer Max Fraser. The New York-based retailer Murray Moss enjoys the provisional atmosphere of exhibitions such as Designers Block, which he compares to medieval markets and which he considers a peculiarly British phenomenon. Their value to him is that they present a relatively unedited selection of design ideas. Most of the exhibits are little more than proposals

and few will ever make it into production, but as such they are free of the obligations of the market. Moss says they have yet to be 'pasteurized' by exposure to the constraints of making a design viable for production. Yet exhibiting proposals means they 'enter the collective consciousness' and will ultimately influence the direction design takes. Moss complains that we impose too many market constraints on products, including furniture, that exist primarily as luxuries. These include maximum functionality, longevity and economy of materials. 'You can demand that of a heart valve, but not of a fruit bowl,' he said, and 'We don't need everything to be so "cured".'[25]

The market for contemporary furniture in Japan has taken its initiative from design trends in Europe and has been led by the entrepreneur Teruo Kurasaki, the man behind the Sputnik and Idée brands who promoted Marc Newson, Michael Young and others early in their careers. More latterly Kurasaki backed Tokyo Designers Block as an umbrella event for contemporary design there, but to date Japan lacks a major trade event or design promotion body to match Europe.

The landscape of furniture has changed since 1990. The industry has become faster and more global, and the market for high-end contemporary design has expanded. Furniture is a major international industry – but it is not just about unit costs, deadlines and spread sheets. Furniture design is redolent of a person or even a nation's taste, aspirations and sense of self-image. It is part of the lifestyle industry and has the capacity to express cultural values as well as to be purely functional.

Twelve case studies of leading figures punctuate the rest of this book, chosen because in my view they have been most influential on the furniture I discuss. Others may disagree with my choice, and everyone will be able to suggest alternative names. The remaining chapters explore stylistic trends since 1990, from salvage and appropriation to functionalism and minimalism, and the gloss of neo-Pop design. Of course designers seldom regard their work within these boundaries, and my chapter themes are merely intended as organizational devices, not as final definitions. The fourth chapter considers furniture in terms of material and technical innovations, both for mass-production and as one-offs, followed by a chapter that examines the role and meaning of conceptual design. The last chapter examines the market for contemporary furniture and its relationship to fashion, the media and the lifestyle industry.

Designers Block, Milan, 2003,
exhibits by Debbie Does and
Flour. Photo: Carlo Draisci.

Tinker chairs, designed
by Ron Arad, edition of six,
manufactured by One Off Ltd,
UK, 1988. Mild steel and stainless
steel. Photo: courtesy of Ron
Arad Associates.

Members of Creative Salvage
at work, about 1984. Photo collage.
V&A: W.680-2001, given by
Mark Brazier-Jones.

Chapter One

Appropriation

*'Have different men arrived?
Men so strong, so powerful that
they can tear sheet metal with
their bare hands as if it were
just little pieces of paper? Men
so powerful that they can take
sheet metal and crumple it,
turn it, fold it from all angles?'* [1]

Ettore Sottsass

The respected Italian designer Ettore Sottsass
wrote this following his first encounter with
Ron Arad's work in the early 1980s, but he
could have been talking about a whole generation of designers and makers, including Tom
Dixon and Danny Lane, who came to prominence at that time. Arad's earliest furniture
was made from salvaged car seats and scaff-
olding systems and, although he rapidly
graduated from using ready-mades, he is often
seen as a figurehead of appropriated design.
This is mostly because his One Off Gallery,
which opened in Neal Street, London, in 1983,
became a focus for many makers. All the new
wave of 'metal bashers' exhibited there, and
architect and designer Nigel Coates eloquently
described it as 'Dr Frankenstein's Furniture
Cave'.[2] Their work was united by their use
of recycled materials and what can best be
described as 'post-industrial chic'. They made
shocking, decadent objects that were urban
and streetwise, filling a space between craft,
art and design, and that stood in deliberate
contrast to the blandness of mainstream furniture. Arad's Tinker chair of 1988, for example
(suitably photographed on the poisoned
docklands wasteland that would host the
Millennium Dome a decade later), looked

mutated, blasted, even post-apocalyptic. Arad
took a different view. 'To me, Post-Apocalyptic
means it should look as though it had been
destroyed, whereas my furniture looks as
if it has just been created.'[3]

From this beginning appropriation
became one of the major means by which
designers challenged the perception and

practice of furniture design that continued
in the 1990s. It encompassed the recycling
of ideas and styles from the past as well as the
reuse of materials. The purpose of appropriation varied too, from being an act of rebellion,
to a pragmatic use of resources, through
to an ethical stance about environmental
sustainability. But it was not a new approach.
Artists and designers throughout the twentieth century had taken things out of context to
make new things. From Marcel Duchamp's
urinal *Fountain* (1917) to Picasso's *Head of a
Bull* (a bicycle seat married to a set of handle-
bars, 1943), it was a small step to Achille and
Pier Giacomo Castiglioni's Mezzadro stool
(made of a tractor seat, 1957).[4] The Castiglionis
legitimized the use of ready-mades and
industrial components in design, and it is
significant that all these designers and artists
were using industrially mass-produced materials and artefacts to create their works. Clearly,

appropriation is a practice that has brought
artists and designers close together. Early
in his career Tom Dixon reported that 'I hate
labels, they are limiting: people are always
anxious to categorize me, but really it depends
on what I am making that week: for example
if it's a comfortable chair then I'm a designer,
but if it's an uncomfortable piece of scrap
metal then I'm an artist.'[5]

Tom Dixon broke down barriers between
art, design and craft, not least because he was
untrained and therefore did not fit into any
preconceived model of practice. In 1984 he
formed Creative Salvage with Mark Brazier-
Jones and Nick Jones, and claimed:

> *We are convinced that the way ahead
> does not lie in expensive, anonymous
> mass-produced hi-tech products. But in
> a more decorative, human approach to
> industrial and interior design. The key
> to Creative Salvage's success is not in
> the expensive research and development
> costs of modern-day products, but in
> the recycling of scrap to form stylish
> and functional artefacts for the home
> and office.*[6]

Untrained and underground, Creative Salvage
was the furniture equivalent of punk, but
instead of discordant music, it threw together
jarring objects out of the detritus of the urban
landscape around it. The same impulse to cut
up and paste together sources from the street
and popular culture could be seen in the contemporary graphics of Jamie Reid, famous for
his ripped and torn graphics for the Sex
Pistols. By the mid-1980s their manager
Malcolm McLaren was amongst the first in
the UK to experiment with musical sampling,
which again was a technique that was compa-
rable to the mixing of objects and materials
adopted by this generation of designers.
Amongst many calls to arms in the Thatcher

MARK   TOM

TOM

Angaraib, designed and made
by Danny Lane, UK, 1987.
Wood boughs, 10mm float glass,
collection of FRAC, Rouen,
France. Photo: Emilio Tremolada.

Victorian chair, designed and
made by Tom Dixon, UK, about
1986. Welded railings, coal-hole
cover and plumbing components.
Photo: courtesy of Phillips,
de Pury & Company.

years was this, from Nigel Coates: 'Don't waste money on trendy glamour objects, exploit the economy of skips and materials fashioned for other uses.'[7] Creative Salvage responded by making objects that were both celebratory in their inventiveness, and funerary in their bleakness. Dixon's Victorian chair not only appropriated identifiable architectural elements (railings, a coal-hole cover) but also the stiff formality of nineteenth-century manners, and evoked the decay of the Victorian terraces of Dixon's Notting Hill home territory. Creative Salvage exhibited on the emerging underground club and gallery scene, and in August 1985 they had a show at the One Off Gallery. Like Ron Arad, Danny Lane and others, Creative Salvage made camera-friendly objects in an age when taste was increasingly led by the media, and the Sunday supplements and emerging 'lifestyle' press, hungry for novelty, did much to popularize the new wave of designers.

Some designers recycled styles to produce furniture in quasi-primitive forms that lent themselves to a massiveness and irregularity that was consciously non-modernist. They were trying to regain the symbolic quality of design that they felt had been obscured by modernism's reductiveness and obsession with functionalism. Of these experiments, the most influential internationally was a collection of furniture and objects by the Italian designer and theorist Andrea Branzi, called 'Domestic Animals' (1985). Branzi sought to 'tame technology' and designed neo-primitive furniture from raw twigs paired with the geometric forms of Italian rationalist design. It was all very ironic, theoretical and uncomfortable. Danny Lane, an erstwhile collaborator with Ron Arad, made furniture from layers of broken glass. Angaraib (1987), made of slivers of glass on salvaged timber supports, was based on a traditional Sudanese sleigh bed. It was evidently less functional than expressive of what furniture could be, and Lane's interests drew him away from furniture towards large-scale public art and architectural commissions. The Israeli-born, Dutch-educated and Swiss-resident designer Natanel Gluska carved one-off massive chairs from solid beechwood using a chainsaw. The shapes were of traditional or even modern chairs, but rendered like this they seemed like ancient thrones or the stone furniture in *The Flintstones* because of the way he made them.[8]

Ironically, neo-primitive furniture was far from simple. It was often highly stylized, decorated or at least decorative and always visually arresting. One such example is the Barbarian range, designed by Elizabeth Garouste and Mattia Bonetti in France (1981). This was made of wrought iron, deliberately coarse, that recalled the archaeological quality of Alberto and Diego Giacometti's cast bronze furniture, as well as finding resonance with furniture by London-based makers such as Arad and André Dubreuil. Garouste and Bonetti's later collections layered styles upon one another, including Wild West, French Empire, Gothic and Asian references, in

Barbarian chair, designed by
Elizabeth Garouste and Mattia
Bonetti, manufactured by Neotu,
France, 1981. Wrought iron,
hide and leather. V&A:
W.4-1994.

true postmodern fashion. They came to represent the more excessive characteristics of 1980s design and seemed increasingly out of step with trends as the 1990s progressed.

André Dubreuil was another French designer who used metal and revived styles to make extraordinary and lavish furniture in the 1980s, but whose work related less to the 1990s. He was taught how to weld by Tom Dixon, making a connection between the British world of Creative Salvage and the French grand tradition his work evoked. Dubreuil revisited baroque furniture for his forms, but modernized them by hammering them from sheet steel, or welded rod. His chairs, consoles, sconces and mirrors seemed fit for the palace of a latter-day Sun King. Like Dubreuil, Philippe Starck often found inspiration in the decorative arts of eighteenth-century France. With characteristic bravura he achieved a triple appropriation with his chair 'Ceci n'est pas une brouette' ('This is not a wheelbarrow', 1995 for French furniture manufacturer XO) which referenced a wheelbarrow, a traditional *fauteuil*, and the 1937 wheelbarrow chair by the Surrealist artist Oscar Dominguez. *Blueprint* was not impressed and described it as his most determined effort in bad taste yet.[9]

The decorative trend did not die out entirely after 1990, but arguably it was no longer leading taste. Creative Salvage had been about rebellion, but quickly it became about exclusivity. After Creative Salvage Mark Brazier-Jones worked less with ready-mades and found components, but increasingly turned to making very luxurious quasi-historicist furniture for a wealthy popstar clientele that included Madonna and Mick Jagger, for whom he reprised French Empire and neo-classical motifs. His Flashman collection of 2003 mixed bizarre Victorian patented furniture with country house style and a suggestion of sadomasochism (a chair called 'Tally Ho' had stirrups like a saddle; it furnished the upmarket Covent Garden erotica store Coco de Mer). Dubreuil and Brazier-Jones were never involved with design for industrial production, and while they could not be described as modernists, neither did they simply reproduce designs and styles of the past. Their works were decadent and luxurious contemporary takes on past styles, and their lavishness set them apart from the cutting-edge as the 1990s progressed. Tom Dixon's career, however, bridged the ebullient statements of 1980s design and the more subdued and ethical design of the 1990s. From his metalwork in the 1980s, Dixon

Paris chair, designed by André
Dubreuil, manufactured by Dubreuil
Decorative Arts, UK, 1988. Waxed
sheet steel with acetylene torch
decoration. V&A: W.8-1989,
given by André Dubreuil.

'Ceci n'est pas une brouette'
armchair, designed by Philippe
Starck, manufactured by XO,
France, 1995. Ash frame, satin
upholstery over foam padding.
Photo: courtesy of XO.

Atlantis armchair, designed and
made by Mark Brazier-Jones, UK,
1989. Cast bronze frame and silk
upholstery. V&A: W.677-2001.

Serbelloni armchair, designed
by Vico Magistretti, manufactured
by De Padova, Italy, 1994. Tubular
steel swivel base, polyurethane
structure, leather upholstery.
Photo: courtesy of De Padova.

Flower-pot table, designed
by Jasper Morrison, 1984,
manufactured by Cappellini,
Italy, 1989. Terracotta flower
pots and glass top. Right
photo: courtesy of Cappellini.
Left photo: Jasper Morrison.

examined other materials. The Bollard chair (1995) was made by reshaping a polyethylene traffic bollard and marked Dixon's departure from recycling and appropriation, and the beginning of experiments with plastics dealt with elsewhere in this book. His work matured into a more sophisticated version of appropriation and his book *Rethink* (2000), like the manifesto for Creative Salvage 15 years earlier, entreated us to consider the functional possibilities of reuse and recycling 'not because it is trendy or wacky, but because it is economic and effective'.[10]

Tom Dixon was in tune with a strand of appropriated design that stretched back to the 1950s and had at its heart an ethical, economic use of materials and means. It was this pragmatic and intelligent use of appropriation, by Italian designers such as Achille Castiglioni (1918-2002), Vico Magistretti (b. 1920) and others, that was to be most influential on the generation of designers after 1990. The old masters themselves were still at work. Castiglioni's Fix bench for De Padova (1994), for example, looked like nothing more than a mattress on an iron trestle, but *Domus* lavished praise, hailing it as 'an ironic anti-bourgeois statement. A true avant-garde "collage", and a veritable Dada experiment.'[11] Magistretti's Incisa chair (1992), and a larger, executive version called Serbelloni (1994),

also for De Padova, were more subtle. They took their inspiration from the stable, like his famous Sindbad chair of 1981, which was inspired by a horse blanket. The chairs' arms and back, made of stitched leather on the outside and lined with quilted cotton, were like a saddle turned through 90 degrees. Importantly they were not literally a saddle, but equally importantly this element of the chair could be made by saddlers, thus keeping alive traditional craft skills that were under threat. Magistretti was concerned that design should maintain a social, sustainable aspect: appropriation and ethics were interconnected.[12]

Inspired by the Castiglioni brothers, Jasper Morrison made a number of ready-mades as a way of imitating some kind of industrial production at a time early in his career when factory resources were not open to him.[13] Mass-produced components must have seemed like a short cut, or at least they short-circuited the division between craft-making and designing for industry. So terra-cotta plant pots stacked in order of size that Morrison saw in a Berlin hardware store became a pedestal base for a table (1984, editioned by Cappellini in 1989). By inserting the bases of two old office chairs into a length of air-conditioning duct, and tapping the raw ends of the metal tubes with wine corks, Morrison created a coat rack (1987, for Aram).

Coatstand, designed and made
by Michael Marriott, UK, 1993.
Beech, beech wood spoons,
chemically treated steel plate.
Photo: Nick Pope.

There was an honesty and simplicity about the way Morrison configured these objects that made the furniture by Dubreuil, Brazier-Jones and the others look mannered and confected. Far from rejecting modernism, as these designers appeared to have done, Morrison was proving Mies van der Rohe's dictum that 'less is more'. Nothing about his furniture was disguised, or superfluous to its function. In this he was like the Castiglioni brothers who took, in 1962, a fishing rod, a transformer and car head lamp to make an uplighter. The results were surreal, intentionally naïve but oddly obvious, and each of us is inspired to think we could have done the same. Appropriation seemed to democratize design because it drew on the visual vocabulary that we all share. It was as if the pool of archetypes and forms had been stirred and a new set of objects drawn from it, each with its own particularities but also universal appeal. On the other hand, might we also regard these assemblages of components as inelegant and clumsy? Is their naivety their strength or their weakness? A generation of designers in the 1990s was convinced it was the former.

This was particularly so of designers in Britain, often linked to the Royal College of Art, where Magistretti was visiting lecturer and from where Morrison had recently graduated. These included Michael Marriott, Jane Atfield, Carl Clerkin, William Warren, and Tord Boontje. In the hardware store they could find beautifully resolved functional objects and components, affordably priced and readily available: like Creative Salvage and Ron Arad, they sought their materials in the urban landscape. Appropriation was the practical answer to the needs of this generation, and was an ethical stance they could embrace. In the early and mid-1990s, around the time they were emerging from the RCA, recycling was widely heralded as the panacea for the over-consumption of the earth's resources. Their objects and furniture, therefore, rapidly gained critical and public acclaim as signifiers of new ways of design and use that would be kinder to the planet.

Much of Michael Marriott's work derived from puns and jokes and he cast himself in the role of design's court jester. From 1989 he made miniature chests of drawers from recycled sardine tins because he wanted to celebrate the high design investment that is generally disregarded in this humble food packaging. Each drawer had a handle made of a length of industrial wire-reinforced hose

and a wing-nut, together evoking the scaly tail of the sardines that were once inside the tins. For SCP, Britain's leading manufacturer of contemporary furniture, he designed a self-assembly coffee table that required a coin to tighten the screws: the coin came with the kit (4x4 table, 1996). For a lampshade, Marriott simply upended a builder's plastic bucket. He explained why:

I chose a bucket because I like its immediacy and familiarity. The idea of making a hole in the bottom of the bucket – making it useless as a bucket – and putting the lightbulb through the hole was very appealing. I made the light by ruining the bucket. I don't see the bucket strictly as a found object, though; I chose it deliberately from the builder's merchant because of its lovely colour. They also do a black bucket which is made from a lower-grade, recycled plastic and it is half the price, but the yellow one is much softer and it gives me the quality of light I was looking for. It's like bananas and custard.[14]

Soft shelves, designed and made by Jane Atfield, UK, 1995. Timber clothes-horse and canvas cover. Photo: courtesy of Jane Atfield.

From his RCA graduation in 1993 Michael Marriott rapidly gained a reputation for his DIY approach to design. His irreverent attitude towards high design, those who design it and those who consume it, captured a new rebellious spirit 10 years after Creative Salvage. Although they both appropriated their source material, Marriott was more inclined towards industrial production of the finished product and more attuned to the ethics of sustainable design. In 1998 he designed the Missed daybed, manufactured by SCP, which ironically evoked a discarded mattress (like Castiglioni's Fix bench) and also a daybed by Mies van der Rohe. With characteristic humour he wanted it to be covered in untreated leather that would gather stains, much like an old mattress. Marriott won the Jerwood Applied Arts Prize for Furniture in 1999 in recognition of the impact his furniture had made in the few years since his graduation, and staged a solo exhibition, 'Mies Meets Marx', at the Geffrye Museum in 2002–3.[15] Since he won the Jerwood Prize Marriott has been less prolific than some of his peers, or than his high profile promised.

Jane Atfield was a year ahead of Marriott at the Royal College of Art, and they shared other common ground: in 1999 she was shortlisted with him for the Jerwood Prize. Like Marriott, Atfield used appropriated content in her furniture; like him she did so to make her designs environmentally sustainable, and because reusable components were the raw materials at hand. Atfield's most significant furniture was made of recycled plastic, and this will be considered elsewhere in this book (see p.95). An early work, while she was still a student, was a chair entirely made of felt specified by the Ministry of Defence to soundproof the inside of tanks, which was suggestive of a Joseph Beuys sculpture. In her other designs she raided the hardware store, the stationery cupboard and the art supplier for those often overlooked components of everyday life. In 1995 she made Soft Shelves, a storage system that co-opted a traditional folding laundry drying rack for its structure. Her screen used wooden school rulers, and her cupboards had artists' canvases on stretchers for doors. Perhaps because Atfield's appropriations seemed to have moved from one part of the room to another, rather than from the street to the home, they do not seek to shock, but gently challenge us to think about the nature of domesticity. The same might be said of Marriott's work. These designers appropriated components for expedience and with wit, rather than

for philosophical musing. More recently Atfield has developed projects with mass-manufacturers, including IKEA, and since 2000 she has collaborated with her husband, painter Robert Shepherd, on printed textiles under the label of Unity Peg.

Carl Clerkin and William Warren design together and independently, and know how difficult it is to persuade manufacturers to make their work. Both studied at the Royal College of Art; Warren studied silversmithing until 1997 and Clerkin graduated from Ron Arad's Design Products course in 1998. One of Clerkin's earliest projects – while he was still a student – was a corkscrew that doubled as a lamp-fitting (1997): an empty wine bottle was co-opted as the lamp base. Another design was for a stool with a handle like a bucket: like Marriott, Clerkin was another habitué of hardware stores. In two joint projects Clerkin and Warren attempted to reinvigorate British manufacturers by designing new objects that reinvented their original products. In this instance appropriation could be regarded as a concern for economic welfare, by contributing to the continuing health and vitality of established British industry. Talco is a company based in the West Midlands that makes metal toolboxes; the designers adapted their standard barn toolboxes (so-called because the profile recalls a barn roof) to become wall-mounted bathroom cabinets (2002). Clerkin and Warren adapted woodworking tools made by Emir in Kent into stylish kitchen implements, such as a meat tenderizer based on a mallet (2001). The aim of both

Rough and Ready collection, designed and made by Tord Boontje, UK, 1998. Timber, army blanket, polypropylene straps, polythene sheet, electric light fittings. Photo: courtesy of Studio Tord Boontje.

Sleeping Rough bed, designed by William Warren UK, 2000. Mahogany. Photo: William Warren.

Talco cabinet, designed by William Warren and Carl Clerkin, manufactured by Talco, 2002. Steel. Photo: William Warren.

You can't lay down your memories
chest of drawers, designed by Tejo
Remy, 1991, made by Tejo Remy
for Droog Design, the Netherlands.
Maple, found drawers, industrial
strap. Collection Droog Design.
Photo: Bob Goedewagen.

collaborations was to add financial value
to anonymous yet highly designed artefacts
by repositioning them in a design-oriented
market. This was an ambitious aim for two
young, independent designers, and despite
a positive critical reception neither project
resulted in products for the market.[16]

By the end of the 1990s, therefore,
appropriation and recycling had gained
social, ethical and environmental credentials.
'Sleeping Rough' was a park bench with an
extended slatted base, creating a bed, designed
by William Warren in 2000. The contradiction of a real bed formed from the site where
vagrants are traditionally forced to camp
out made a bold political statement about the
reality of homelessness. Other designers used
appropriation for political and social ends too.

Tord Boontje's 'Rough and Ready' collection
of chairs, lights, tables and storage units in
1998 felt like furniture created in a state of
emergency. Variously described as 'brutal and
civilized' and as having 'no industry, no mystery', the collection was made of the crudest
materials and begged the question 'what kind
of society do we live in where these are necessary?'.[17] The pieces were roughly constructed
from unfinished, cheap timber sections using
basic carpentry skills, not cabinet-making
techniques. The cupboard was faced with
polythene sheeting edged with masking tape
and the chair was finished with a second-
hand army blanket lashed over the timber
frame with polypropylene strapping usually
used for sealing cardboard cartons. They were
not intended to be beautiful, only expedient.
'These are the materials you could find in a
skip,' said Boontje. 'Too much energy is wasted
putting things together in contrived ways.
The aim of this is to show that you can make
a perfectly good chair by reutilising what
exists already.'[18] As if to prove his point he
published the design so anyone could make
it. His Rough and Ready furniture was gen-
uinely shocking because the materials were
so poor, and the message of the furniture
was so pertinent.

Lashing things together, and crudely
joining components, is a very simple and
expressive method of making furniture.[19]
As Boontje showed (and Morrison before
him), it is an honest way to construct an
object because it is undisguised and pragmatic.
Components are kept visually separate, and
seams and joins are revealed and celebrated
(in direct contrast to the sleek and seamless
so-called 'Blobjects' that will be discussed
elsewhere; see p.75). In 1989 Danny Lane
made the Woodcutter's Table from timber
off-cuts. This was a broad disk of variously
sized chunks of wood with a common surface
height, bound tightly by a massive rusted
iron chain around the circumference. Patrik
Fredrikson reprised and refined the same
idea in 2002 for a table made of raw birch
logs, complete with bark, bound by an industrial steel strap. It was primitive because
the wood was raw (Fredrikson described
it as 'archaic'), but without the ostentation
of Garouste and Bonetti's Barbarian furniture.

Outside Britain, young designers were
using similar means, but appropriation was
more about conveying concepts than making-
do-and-mending. The most iconic piece
of 'lashed-together' furniture was Tejo Remy's
chest of drawers called 'You can't lay down
your memories' (1991), which he made from

Table #1, designed by Patrik Fredrikson, manufactured by Fredrikson Stallard, UK, 2002. Untreated birch, steel strap. Photo: Fredrikson Stallard.

various mismatched and discarded drawers from old pieces of furniture. Each drawer was encased in a new timber carcase and the whole group was encircled by a fabric strap like those used to secure loads on heavy goods vehicles. The arbitrariness of the odd drawers and the accidental angles they assume in the new configuration were moderated by their pristine new housings. The provisional quality of the ensemble was intentional, but did Remy really intend the strap to be loosened, and the group re-arranged? The misaligned drawers were not very useful, but as its name suggests it was less about function than about the emotions it evoked, which was the memory of the cupboards from which these various drawers came, and of what they contained in their former life. This elegiac quality pervaded much subsequent Dutch design, particularly that associated with Droog Design from 1993, and specifically work by Jurgen Bey, and 'You can't lay down your memories' was one of the first designs that Droog Design editioned.[20] Remy used straps for his Rag chair too (1991, also later editioned by Droog Design), but this time they were steel. The Rag chair's upholstery was discarded textile, bundled around a wooden structure, with the appearance of a fabric bale. Both Remy and Boontje exploited the contrast of the industrial straps against the softness of the fabric.

Across Europe designers have appropriated discarded objects and also archetypes and design classics, to make new objects. Uwe Fischer and Klaus-Achim Heine formed Ginbande in Frankfurt in 1985 (disbanded 1995), and in the same year they exhibited at the One Off Gallery. A project for children's furniture in 1991 played with elements of a bentwood chair. In one piece, three chair backs supported an upholstered ring. In another, the front legs and the edge of the seat appeared to emerge from a table top.[21] The designers made reference to a ubiquitous, placeless and timeless chair similar to a design produced continuously since 1916 by the Swiss manufacturer Horgen Glarus. In 2000 the Horgen Glarus chair became the subject of a new work by N2, four young Swiss designers (Paolo Fasulo, Christian Deuber, Jörg Boner and Kuno Nüssli). They replaced the moulded plywood seat with a translucent acrylic panel fitted with a circular fluorescent tube. Now the chair was also a lamp. By this simple intervention the appropriated design was given a new function. N2 called their chair Pof 1, meaning 'piece of furniture', alluding to the archetypal and non-specific nature of the chair/lamp. The piece was part of the collection by the short-lived Dutch company, Hidden, and shares traits with Dutch design.[22] Both Ginbande and

N2 had appropriated similar archetypal chairs: Ginbande quoted elements of the chair's structure, and N2 manipulated the structure to make a new object. Jurgen Bey used a similar archetypal bentwood chair for his Kokon furniture (1997) and another version appeared as Peter Traag's Mummy chair for Edra in 2005.

Almost all the furniture discussed so far was made as one-offs or in very small batches, but ideas surrounding appropriation reached broader markets. Philippe Starck is such a prolific designer of products and furniture that his avowed concern for the environment can ring hollow. Yet since the late 1980s he has used his position as the world's most famous furniture designer to speak loudly about the need to use less and use it better. By 1991 he could claim: 'My main ambition – no, production – this year has been to design with NO STYLE. For many years we all sought style. Now we need discretion, something invisible, something that provides a real service for people, a really generous idea, affordable, not too heavy for mobility. With a good product, there is no obligation to show its design.'[23] Starck wanted to downplay the evidence of his hand in the design, and he did this by appropriating styles from the past. It was as if he was trying to subsume his personality as a designer in the borrowed history of furniture design and archetypes. The Dutch designer Richard Hutten looked to archetypal forms for similar reasons, describing his approach as 'no sign of design'. Starck's Hudson (2000) and Heritage (2001) chairs for Emeco were subtle reworkings of the American manufacturer's classic Model 1006 all-aluminium chair. Miss Sisi was the name he gave to a small plastic light that looked like a cartoon drawing of a lamp: it was deliberately anonymous and ubiquitous. And with a range of chairs for Kartell, such as Louis Ghost, Starck reworked the shapes of eighteenth-century French chairs in plastic. Starck aimed to add value to his products, and render them timeless, by connecting them to historic, commonly accepted styles and forms.

Most of these designers respected or even revered their appropriated sources. Maarten Baas, on the other hand, perversely refreshed our perception of archetypal objects by setting fire to them and preserving their remains with epoxy.[24] Like fellow Dutch designers, Baas traded in memory, nostalgia and a warped view of bourgeois values. The furniture he burnt was all familiar, either generically, as with the reproduction period pieces shown in Milan and subsequently manufactured by Moooi (see page 120) or as design classics, such as the 25 pieces shown at Moss, New York, in the summer of 2004.[25] These included Tejo Remy's chest of drawers, as well as furniture by the Eameses, Mackintosh, Rietveld, Sottsass and Gaudi, and contemporary designs by Richard Hutten and the Campana brothers. Since Baas contributed no design to these pieces, it is debatable whether they were works of design or of art. Appropriation had become a conceptual stance. The Smoke collection was undoubtedly shocking because it confronted us with violent despoliation. Baas symbolically destroyed the recent history of design in order to draw a line under it. Memphis overturned modernism, Droog Design superseded Memphis, then Baas took iconic pieces from all twentieth-century avant-gardes and burnt them. It was the logical conclusion and apotheosis of appropriation, as the designer destroyed that which he had appropriated.

Pof 1 chair, designed by N2, manufactured by Hidden, the Netherlands, 2000. Bent beech, acrylic and electric light component. V&A: W.667-2001, given by Hidden.

Where There's Smoke, 15/05/2004, made by Maarten Baas, the Netherlands, 2004. Burnt Carlton room divider, designed by Ettore Sottsass for Memphis, 1981. Photo: Maarten van Houten.

Jurgen Bey

Tree Trunk bench, designed for the Droog Design Couleur Locale project. Untreated log with cast bronze chair backs, 1999. Collection Droog Design. Photo: Marsel Loermans.

'A designer can never be original. Everything I use or apply comes from the existing world. I simply give it a personal touch but I don't invent anything. A designer's greatest achievement is to change the perspective of things a little.' [1]

Jurgen Bey takes things he finds around him and makes furniture and objects that are little essays in nostalgia and memory. Generally he chooses things that are ubiquitous or obsolete; bentwood café chairs, for example, or old crockery and lamps. Either way, these objects are all but invisible in contemporary culture, which is obsessed with newness and novelty. In various ways Bey restores and revives his old objects, making them useful again but also drawing our attention back to them.

The Kokon furniture was a series of broken-down old chairs and tables that Bey, with Jan Konings, designed in 1997. They were part of a project called 'Dry Tech' initiated by Droog Design with the Aviation and Space Laboratory of Delft University. The furniture was overlaid with spun PVC, a high-tech coating that shrunk around the skeleton to make a new skin, literally cocooning it. The chairs appeared to be bandaged

and there is an allusion to protection, to making good. Bey used the same allusion for the Broken Family tea service that comprised mismatched, chipped and discarded junk-shop tableware. He emphasized its worth by unifying the group with a new gilt coating, making what had been rubbish into something fragile, precious and beautiful, literally and metaphorically restoring its (bourgeois) value.

One of Jurgen Bey's most famous designs was for the Light Shade shade (1999). Again, an existing object was resurfaced. This time he chose what some might regard as tasteless old table lamps, which he encased in shiny, reflective new polyester foil cylinders. They were made all the more odd because Bey converted them into pendant lights. When the lamps were switched off they were invisible, but switched on they appeared through the foil like ghostly evocations of themselves, table lamps mysteriously elevating in the control of poltergeists, perhaps. Bey was wrapping up the past, protecting and sequestering the object and all the memories attached to it. By making familiar, discarded objects unfamiliar and strange, he drew our attention to their values. He was not only recycling artefacts, but also keeping continuity with the past.

At times the designer's hand is very slight. The Healing Project (1999) restored purpose and meaning to broken furniture – for example, a stack of books simply propped up a broken chair: the detached leg itself found new life as a child's toy. The designer intervened so far, no further, and his intervention was clearly expressed. The same economy of means characterized the use of a log to make the Tree Trunk bench, although it was not Bey's choice to inset it with Victorian chair-backs cast in bronze, a material redolent of high sculpture.

Jurgen Bey, therefore, seems to recycle old furniture and styles to remind us of the value of the past. Does this make him a neo-conservative, looking over his shoulder rather than forward into the future? He appropriates petit bourgeois symbols such as rococo revival tea sets and parlour chairs, but with irony, gently mocking our nostalgia for the certainties of history. His designs are theatrical, camp even, but they speak eloquently. 'Everything has a voice and speaks its own language,' he said. 'And so design is also a language, subject to rules.'[2]

Lightshade shade, two-way mirror foil, existing lamp, 1999. Collection Droog Design. Photo: courtesy of Droog Design.

Kokon furniture, designed for the Droog Design Dry Tech project. PVC coating over existing furniture, 1997. Photo: Bob Goedewagen.

Marcel Wanders

Crochet table, manufactured
by Moooi, the Netherlands, 2001.
Cotton, epoxy. Photo: Maarten
Van Houten.

Pebbles storage container/stool,
manufactured by Magis, Italy,
2000. High-impact polystyrene
(Styrolux®). Photo: Carlo
Lavatori.

*'It's not recycling the material
or the ready-made aspect
that interests me. What does
is the re-use of the archetype,
the recycling of the idea. This
is because I want to make
products that are well-worn
favourites even when being
first introduced.'* [1]

One of Dutchman Marcel Wanders' earliest
designs was merely a stack of archetypal
shades to make a lamp (Set Up Shades, 1988),
and was selected for the first Droog Design
collection. He chooses archetypal forms,
familiar materials and traditional techniques
because they are recognizable and carry associations with them, such as macramé, knitting
and basketwork. But then he subverts them,
and by making familiar things seem strange
he invites us to look more closely at them
and at our preconceptions. The Knotted chair
(1996, see page 100), which is probably his
best-known design, asks us to believe that
pliable macramé can be structural and stiff.
Our senses no longer agree with our preconceptions. In 2001 Cappellini produced a chromed version of the chair that added another
layer to our incredulity: now it looked like
it had been knotted from solid metal. The
Crochet table (2000) also transforms a familiar
technique. There is a homeliness to this table
that derives from associations with knitting
and home production, yet here the knitting
is stiffened and structural. The Willow chair
was designed for the Droog Design project
'Couleur Locale' (1999), for which designers
proposed objects that would help regenerate
the economy, and enhance the environment,
of Oranienbaum in eastern Germany.
Wanders' chair updated traditional wicker
chairs and was intended to be made by
a basket-maker on the estate of the Oranienbaum Palace.

Wanders says he wants to design 'objects
that touch you and that generate a positive
feeling. In short, objects worth bonding with
for a lifetime.' [2] It is a concern he shares with
other Dutch designers. Not all his furniture

features traditional craft techniques, but each object has a distinct personality. Wanders styled the VIP room of the Dutch Pavilion at the Hanover World Expo in 2000 to look like an ice-rink in a woodland grove and included 44 compact wool-covered armchairs. The VIP chair wears flared 'trousers' that conceal castors and give the effect of it gliding on air, or skating on ice. Though designed for a specific location, subsequently the chair entered production with the Dutch firm Moooi, of which Wanders is Creative Director. The firm is significant because it has commercialized the conceptual approach to design advocated by Droog Design. Wanders designs many of the products himself, but also includes objects by others, among them Joep van Lieshout, Ross Lovegrove, Constantin and Laurene Leon Boym and Jeffrey Bernett. Wanders also designs for other manufacturers, notably the Italians Cappellini and Magis, for whom he designed a wheeled plastic storage-box-cum-stool called 'Pebble' in 2000. Perhaps more than his furniture, Wanders' experiments with ceramics and rapid prototyping have pushed the boundaries of product design – for example, the Sponge Vase (1997) made by firing a slip-soaked sea sponge, and the Airborne Snotty Vase (2001), the shape of which was generated from a 3D-scan of a drop of mucus. Inventiveness and irreverence run throughout Marcel Wanders' designs. When invited to contribute to Gijs Bakker's prestigious 'Chi ha Paura...?' jewellery collection, who else would propose a solid gold clown's nose?

Willow chair, woven by Steffan Kolbe in Oranienbaum, Germany, for the Droog Design Couleur Locale project, 1999, wicker. Photo: Marsel Loermans.

VIP chair, manufactured by Moooi, the Netherlands, 2000. Timber frame with wool upholstery. Photo: Maarten Van Houten.

Chapter Two

New Functionalism

'I was in Milan. I can remember a kind of cold sweat at the opening. I went with religious dedication to the fair in Milan every year, and that Memphis opening, I don't know how I got in, but I got in and, uhm, I can remember, the sort of feeling of shock and panic like: "It's already happened!"... It was the weirdest feeling: you were in one sense repulsed by the objects, or I was, but also immediately freed by the sort of total rule-breaking.'[1]

Jasper Morrison

This was how Jasper Morrison, who was to become the figurehead of a pared down, functionalist movement in furniture design in the 1990s, recalled his repulsion for Memphis in 1981, while acknowledging its liberating effect. To Morrison, its 'decorative uselessness' represented 'a "closed" style that led nowhere'.[2] What reasons were there for a quest for simplicity, anonymity and modernity in furniture design?

Economic factors undoubtedly played their part. The 1980s had been the decade of corporate raids and stock-market boom and bust, epitomized by Gordon Gekko in Oliver Stone's movie *Wall Street* and Sherman McCoy, one of Tom Wolfe's 'Masters of the Universe' in *The Bonfire of the Vanities*, both from 1987. But that same year, Monday 19 October became known as 'Black Monday', the greatest stock-market fall in history, rocking world markets. Economic confidence was shaken and began to be replaced by economic caution: the 1990s were to be more straitened times. Perhaps this was reflected in a swing in taste away from exuberance towards sobriety. Design and interiors writer Nonie Niesewand recognized that 'Memphis is the cult of the decade that made the crossover into public consciousness - never was so little appreciated by so many.'[3] It had become so closely identified with the values and aesthetics of its era that it could not survive changing times and in the summer of 1988 Ettore Sottsass quietly announced that Memphis, in its original form, was over too.[4]

As world economies sank into recession, furniture design reflected a new spirit of parsimony and modesty, in parallel with John Major's call for 'back to basics' British politics. By 1993 critics in Italy and in the UK were talking about the New Functionalists, a group of designers and manufacturers who espoused anonymity and functionality above all else, singling out Jasper Morrison and the Italian firm of Cappellini as its leaders. Simplified, plain and functional furniture dominated the

catalogues of manufacturers in Sweden, Italy and Britain, and the studios of designer-makers and architect-artists in the low countries and the United States. Beyond the economic imperative, simplified furniture design was inspired by fine art and architecture, notably the sculpture and design of Donald Judd and the minimalist buildings of architects such as John Pawson, Claudio Silverstrin and Tadao Ando. An architectural and reductive approach to design and construction was common to all this furniture, from Judd right through to the mass-market offerings of IKEA.

Judd made furniture from the 1960s to his death in 1994. It was an extension of his sculpture, he was unconstrained by a manufacturer's brief, and he never needed to sell his furniture to survive, but nevertheless Judd intended his furniture to be used, and he lived with it himself. It shared space in his homes in New York and Marfa, Texas with his collection of early modern furniture by Gerrit Rietveld (to whom it is most indebted) and Alvar Aalto. Judd's designs struck a chord with many furniture designers, and Ron Arad explained his appeal: Judd 'went a step further than the 1950s people [the Eameses *et al.*], and stripped the chair of industrial sense, or industrial common sense. Stripped of comfort, ergonomics, anything like that. And yet it answered the necessary condition to be a chair. Or in the case of his other design works, to be a table.'[5] John Pawson relished the unforgiving quality of the furniture, but also noted that staff

Donald Judd Architecture Office, Marfa, Texas, including (from front to back): Table #73, #75 and #74, fabricated by Pro Raum, Cologne, 1990, birch plywood; Standing Writing Desk #78, fabricated by Wood and Plywood Furniture, New York, 1993, birch plywood; Chair #84/5, fabricated by Wood and Plywood Furniture New York, 2 red 1992, 1 green 1991, Finland colour plywood; Library Chair and Stool #42, fabricated by Cooper/Kato, New York, 1984, elm; collection of Judd Foundation. Photo: © Judd Foundation 2006 / Judd Works.

in his office would fight to use a Judd chair 'not just for a brief trial, but to sit on for a whole day at the drawing board.'[6] Andreas Brandolini, who had previously taught Jasper Morrison at the Hochschule in Berlin during his sabbatical from the Royal College of Art, created box-like chairs made from rough-hewn timber in the late 1980s, very similar in character to Judd's uncompromising furniture.

Donald Judd's influence was most profoundly evident in the work of Belgian designer Maarten Van Severen. Both explored the intersection of planes and lines at right angles, and the rhythm of solids and voids, and they shared a sense for proportions and a common vocabulary of materials. But Van Severen did not claim to be making art, and neither he nor Judd tried to impose meanings onto their furniture. In this they ran against the overtly symbolic character of postmodern design that was laden with meanings ascribed

by the designer. They believed their furniture just was what it was, or as Arad put it, it answered the necessary conditions to be furniture. Architecture and design writer Geert Bekaert explored this further: Van Severen 'makes things that people call furniture, that also claim the status of works of art, that refer to architecture, that recall minimalism and maximalism, and much more besides, but which make it clear first and foremost that those terms are no more than pseudonyms adopted in order to be able to exist in our world.'[7] His furniture seemed inscrutable and indifferent to its surroundings, placeless and timeless, and he achieved this by a reductive process that left only the material, often oak, plywood or aluminium, in a raw, self-coloured state. Designers who appropriated their components often left them and their joins visible, as a sign of the honesty of the object, but Van Severen deliberately concealed all signs of

Low chair, designed by Maarten
Van Severen, 1993-5, manufactured
by MaartenVanSeverenMeubelen,
Belgium, 2001. Aluminium. V&A:
W.669-2001, given by Top Mouton.

structure so meanings or values could not
be imposed on his furniture. Because of his
strenuous efforts to simplify he preferred
to be thought of as a maximalist rather than
a minimalist. His extremely plain chairs
and long tables were somehow monastic,
and his interiors were suggestive of medieval
refectories. In this he was like Richard
Hutten, another designer of attenuated tables.
Hutten's café for the Centraal Museum in
Utrecht was actually sited in the refectory
of a former monastery, and Van Severen
designed a bar for a former abbey in Ghent.
Both rooms were redolent of Calvinistic
frugality and humility. Certainly there is
a 'deliberate ascetism' and 'a silent quality'
(both Bekaert) to Van Severen's work that
is the silence of meditation, not absence.

Van Severen studied architecture before
turning to furniture, which may explain its
monumentality. Only in his chairs did Van
Severen use curves (and then only seldomly),
the most famous being Chair No. 2 (1992),
designed first totally in aluminium, then as an
aluminium frame for a plywood shell. There
was a provisional quality to this chair derived
from a simple device. The front legs were
oblong-sectioned extensions of the chair's
frame and the plane of the seat and back, but
the rear legs were round-sectioned and looked
like temporary props placed there to stop the
chair falling backwards. All sign of the joints
between the legs and the seat were concealed
or erased. In 1998 Vitra successfully translated
this chair for industrial production in polyurethane foam stiffened with internal steel
springs, renaming it 'Chair .03'. Further
variations were launched after Van Severen's
death in 2005.

Two versions of Chair No.2 (1992), and Low chair (1993), designed by Maarten Van Severen, manufactured by MaartenVanSeverenMeubelen, Belgium. Aluminium, beech and beech plywood. V&A: W.670, 671, 672-2001, given by Top Mouton.

Until the mid-1990s Van Severen made his own furniture, but this was not cost-effective. In 1994, for example, he only made 20 wooden tables, 20 aluminium tables, 50 chairs and some shelves and cabinets, all to commission and all painstakingly by hand.[8] In 1998 Top Mouton, Belgium's most respected interiors firm, took over production of the MaartenVanSeverenMeubelen™ collection.[9] The designer concentrated on furniture that could be manufactured commercially, by Vitra and Bulo, both office furniture specialists for whom his minimalist style was appropriate.

In 1995 the architect Philipp Mainzer and product designer Florian Asche, graduates of Central Saint Martins, founded E15, named after the postcode of the East London district of Stratford where they were first based. Their furniture is generally made of solid oak or walnut, or folded aluminium sheet, and is monumental and architectonic, much like Van Severen's work. The look of E15 furniture is modern, but the materials and craftsmanship are traditional. The Belgian designer Hans de Pelsmacker's slab-like combined

table and seating is a good example of the company's output.

Minimalist art and architecture, therefore, were influences on the prevailing trend towards simplified furniture in the 1990s, and so was a reappraisal of modernism. The ubiquity of modernist forms in the corporate sphere, combined with the social and structural failures of modernist architecture in the 1960s and the arrival of postmodern architectural theories in the 1970s, meant that by the 1980s modernist design was largely perceived at worst as a failure and at best as dogmatic and rather dull. As early as the 1960s, however, Cassina (and other, lesser, Italian manufacturers) had begun to rehabilitate the reputations of modernist pioneers by reissuing their furniture some 30 years after it was designed and in greater numbers than ever were produced before World War II. Furniture designs by figures such as Marcel Breuer, Mies van der Rohe, Le Corbusier, Eileen Gray and their followers now enjoyed popularity amongst a small band of like-minded fans, mostly architects or designers. Quite possibly a degree

of hero-worshipping and myth-making played its part here too. In Britain the influential retailer Zeev Aram worked with Eileen Gray near the end of her life to make commercial editions of her furniture that previously had only existed as one-offs or small editions for specific interiors. These included the Bibendum chair and the side table from her house E-1027, and each year from 1975 Aram introduced a new piece. In 1979, three years after her death, the Victoria and Albert Museum staged an exhibition of Gray's work. This exhibition (and others such as 'The Thirties' at the Hayward Gallery, also in 1979), were part of the rehabilitation of pre-war modernism in the public consciousness. Jasper Morrison recalled that seeing the Eileen Gray exhibition, aged about 16, made him realize he wanted to be a furniture designer: 'I saw a language which I could relate to and which I understood.'[10]

It was no coincidence, therefore, that Zeev Aram and Sheridan Coakley, Morrison's first supporters, were fellow fans of modernism. Aram was the first to exhibit Morrison's Thinking Man's chair (1986) made, like much modernist furniture, from tubular metal. Giulio Cappellini saw it there and subsequently assumed production.[11] Coakley was a dealer of early twentieth-century furniture, before licensing the manufacture of 1930s modernist designs by PEL (Practical Equipment Ltd) in the early 1980s. In 1985 he gained the rights to distribute Philippe Starck's chairs just as the Frenchman was becoming a design superstar. In the same year he formed SCP to manufacture new designs and Jasper Morrison was one of his first signings. 'I've always agreed with modernist principles,' Coakley once said, 'I find it hard now to deviate from them.'[12] Coakley was an early champion of Konstantin Grcic too, whom he admired for his 'good Bauhaus approach'. Jasper Morrison introduced them at Grcic's RCA degree show in 1990 and very quickly Grcic was designing for SCP. His earliest furniture, such as the Tam-Tam and Tom-Tom side tables (1991), were blocky and unadorned. The Knight and Bishop dining tables (1991), also for SCP, had chunky solid beech bases that recalled joinery while also paying homage to Gerrit Rietveld's constructive manner.

More than anyone else in Britain, Sheridan Coakley was the chief promoter of New Functionalist furniture, and he assembled a group of mostly young designers who quickly gained international reputations. Alongside Morrison and Grcic, these

numbered Matthew Hilton, Terence Woodgate, James Irvine, Andrew Stafford and Michael Marriott. Coakley encouraged and enabled each designer to develop his own distinct style, but all SCP furniture was informed by Coakley's adherence to the functionalism of modernist design principles. 'Sheridan *is* Britain's contemporary furniture industry', Terence Woodgate once observed, and though there may be more small design-led manufacturers in Britain today, in the 1990s SCP was the only company with a vision and the skills to produce furniture that could compete internationally. SCP remained a relatively small company, but punched above its weight, enjoying considerable influence outside Britain; Giulio Cappellini remarked that 'Sheridan would be rich and famous if he worked in Milan and not London.'[13]

Terence Woodgate's reductive design, springing from his understanding of engineering and materials, was typical of SCP's furniture. Like Morrison, Woodgate reduced the forms and elements of each piece to their minimum to achieve what one critic described as 'a sense of poised serenity'.[14] His public seating of 1994 opened up the contract market to SCP and introduced a harder edge to New Functionalism, inspired by engineering and High-Tech architecture. It was shortlisted for Norman Foster's Chek Lap Kok airport in Hong Kong (1992–8). Woodgate went on to design storage and seating for Cappellini and the Spanish manufacturer Punt Mobles

Thinking Man's chair, designed by Jasper Morrison, manufactured by Cappellini, Italy, 1986. Painted tubular and sheet steel. V&A: W.15-1989, given by Aram Designs Ltd.

Sofa, designed by Jasper Morrison, manufactured by SCP, UK, 1988. Cotton and linen upholstery over foam padding, steel springs, hessian and elasticized webbing on beech frame, aluminium feet, feather cushions. V&A: W.16-1990, given by SCP Ltd.

HP01 table bench, designed by Hans de Pelsmacker, manufactured by E15, Germany, 2000. Oiled oak. Photo: courtesy of E15.

in the mid-1990s, but remained a regular SCP designer too. An interplay of geometric purity and freeform curves appeared in his designs, and in the best work of Jasper Morrison. In Morrison's plywood chair for Vitra (1989), for example, the rigidly square seat and front legs were counterbalanced by the sensual curves of the rear legs that suggested both the human form and the structure of stringed instruments. Woodgate's design was less poetic than Morrison's, and more engineered, but both were masters at humanizing functionalist design without over-embellishing their furniture. Both designed softer, more welcoming furniture than anything by Van Severen.

James Irvine's career echoes Morrison's: he was a year ahead of Morrison at the RCA, graduating in 1984, and in the 1990s he designed furniture for Sheridan Coakley too. Irvine was a conduit between the London furniture designers and Italy, because he had moved to Milan in 1984 to work first for Olivetti then in the office of Ettore Sottsass. Morrison was a frequent visitor. Milan remained the centre of the contemporary furniture industry but, increasingly, advanced

design ideas were coming from outside Italy. Giulio Cappellini was the first Italian manufacturer to pick up on the new wave of promising designers coming from London, and in 1991 he was the first manufacturer to make James Irvine's furniture.

In 1987 Blueprint reported that 'perhaps it is weathercocks like Cappellini, who adopt a scattergun stylistic approach, that provide the clearest insight into the way things are going', acknowledging the company's position at the vanguard of furniture design development.[15] Founded in 1946, by the 1990s Cappellini was a distinctive, trend-setting brand, the furniture equivalent of fellow Milanese high-fashion labels such as Armani and Versace. Giulio Cappellini trained as an architect and joined the family firm in 1979. His vision for the company in the 1990s was clear. He wanted to blend overtly 'designed', sculptural furniture such as Tom Dixon's 'S' chair and pieces by Marc Newson with the understated furniture of Jasper Morrison, James Irvine, Thomas Eriksson and Thomas Sandell.[16] This was also a response to the difficult economic climate, and part of his strategy involved introducing lower-cost furniture

Tam-Tam and Tom-Tom side tables, designed by Konstantin Grcic, manufactured by SCP, UK, 1991. Painted steel and wood. Photo: courtesy of KGID.

Tables designed by James Irvine for the Progetto Oggetto collection, manufactured by Cappellini, Italy, 1992. Laminate and anodized aluminium. Photo: courtesy of Cappellini.

Charles Large sofa, designed by
Antonio Citterio, manufactured
by B&B Italia, Italy, 1997.
Steel frame, aluminium feet,
polyurethane foam, polyester
wadding, down, fabric or leather
upholstery. Photo: courtesy
of B&B Italia.

Elevenfive storage system, designed
by Bruno Fattorini, manufactured
by MDF Italia, Italy, 2004. Lacquered
wood. Photo: courtesy of MDF Italia.

that would compete with the cheaper
fashionable furniture that was undercutting
the market; a phenomenon Italian manufacturers dubbed 'the IKEA effect'.[17] Cappellini
developed Ross Lovegrove's Figure of Eight
chair to compete in the aggressive market for
low-cost plastic chairs, but it was not a particular success. More successful for the company
was the introduction of Progetto Oggetto in
1992, a range of 'necessary and not so necessary
objects' for the home, under the artistic
direction of Jasper Morrison and James Irvine.
The collections included Thomas Eriksson's
'Red Cross' medicine cabinet and Morrison's
bottles, and these objects sum up the design
intent of the project. These were designed
with self-aware simplicity and a sense of
two-dimensionality: they were almost graphic
representations of themselves, where their
materiality was distilled to the point at which
they became logos. The collection may have
appeared to comprise 'necessary objects'
but it was pitched at the high-end market
of Cappellini's core consumer group who
would pay premium prices for design objects.
Cappellini did not differentiate between
elite prices and useful objects and ultimately,
for this firm, New Functionalism only
meant new fashion.

Cappellini was not the only Italian
to promote New Functionalism. Claudio
Lazzarini and Carl Pickering's Dormusa bed

system (1994) comprised vertical and horizon-
tal plank structures intersecting each other
in an architectonic way, but producing a
luxurious rather than an ascetic effect, recalling Frank Lloyd Wright more than Tadao
Ando. Amongst manufacturers MDF (Modern
Design Furniture) was the most thorough
Italian exponent of minimalist furniture.
Luxuriously glossy storage and seating,
much of it designed by Bruno Fattorini in
aluminium or other metals, was reduced
to the most simplified, graphic terms.

B&B Italia (founded as C&B Italia in
1969) had grown into one of the largest and
most influential Italian manufacturers by
the 1990s, and its success primarily arose
from collaboration with the designer Antonio
Citterio, dating back to 1975. Citterio was
untouched by the pomp and bluster of the
Milanese design scene of the late 1970s and
1980s. His architecture and furniture designs
(at different times in collaboration with
Paola Nava and Glen Oliver Löw) remained
rational, engineered and pared-down. Citterio
designed furniture that looked weightless,
comprising volumes reduced to geometric
forms and intersecting planes, distillations
of his modernist architectural principles.
His furniture, therefore, was in keeping with
the simplicity of minimalism and the humility
of the New Functionalists. Citterio was
a minimalist by temperament, rather than
fashion, his minimalism arose from engineering and his designs often celebrated the highly
industrialized techniques used to make them.
Rather like Judd or Van Severen, he was not
interested in the symbolism of the furniture,
but in reducing it to its elemental constituent
parts.[18] This is clearly so with a series of sofas
designed for B&B Italia since the 1970s that
appear to defy gravity. They were generally
very low and sprawling, like architectural
compositions, supported on spindly metal
legs. The look became the prevailing shape
of the sofa for the 1990s and was much
emulated, for example by Piero Lissoni for
the manufacturer Living Divani, and by many
other companies across Europe.

Cappellini included Swedish designers
alongside the British when he looked for
talent outside Italy, and through the 1990s
Sweden was to regain much of the kudos
Scandinavian designers had enjoyed
internationally in the 1950s. The new spirit
of functionalism that was appearing in
London and Milan fitted with the tradition
of Scandinavian modernism. The larger and
established firms such as Källemo, Offecct
and Lammhults made furniture in the

Swecode advertisement,
Blueprint, 125, February 1996.

Hockney sofa, designed by Eero
Koivisto, manufactured by David
Design, Sweden, 1999. Metal
and wood frame, polyurethane
foam padding, fabric upholstery.
Photo: courtesy of David Design.

fastidious and functionally oriented Swedish tradition. There were several small, independent design-led manufacturers too, helping to build the careers of younger designers. For example, the designers Thomas Sandell and Tom Hedqvist, the Principal of Beckmans Design School, formed Element in the early 1990s with the buzzwords 'basic, beautiful, humorous, fun and lustful', to market furniture and objects for the home and office. In spirit it was akin to Cappellini's Progetto Oggetto, though Hedqvist dismissed the Italian collection as 'nothing but an extension of the cult of the designer as star, an Italian phenomenon, an international item mania, aimed at wealthy customers.'[19] In 1995 Stefan Ytterborn, a design brand manager, brought together five small Swedish manufacturers to exhibit internationally under the banner of 'Swecode' (Swe[dish] Co[ntemporary] De[sign]). The products of all five companies - CBI, Asplund, BOX, Forminord and David Design - shared common characteristics, not least because some designers, such as Sandell, were designing for several members of the group. The companies shared a philosophy too, summed up by CBI as 'humanism, respect for natural materials, comfort, function, availability and the user in focus'.[20] The furniture was not radically or wilfully minimal, but tended towards a 'politesse' and refinement that has always characterized Swedish design.

Mårten Claesson, Eero Koivisto and Ola Rune all graduated from Konstfack (the University College of Art, Crafts and Design, Stockholm) in 1994. By the end of the decade they were designing, together and individually, for David Design, the member of Swecode with arguably the most commercially developed range of products. Together they produced the Bowie chair and ottoman (1998) in moulded plywood and sheepskin, which recalled mid-century Danish furniture. Eero Koivisto followed Citterio with his extremely long and low Hockney sofa system (1999). David Carlson, who founded David Design in 1988, likes to name his furniture after other famous Davids, and the catalogue includes objects called Niven, Blaine, Craig, Byrne, Bailey and Lynch. Björn Dahlström is a highly regarded industrial designer who enjoyed a close association with the manufacturer CBI. He designed an upholstered side chair for the company in 1994 that was little more than a padded comma on four timber blocks. It spawned a group of thick-seated designs for CBI that exploited the volume of the upholstery, rather than attempting to reduce its presence. Another family of chairs had extra-wide seats, sometimes pierced with hand grips, that updated the classic shapes of Arne Jacobsen's plywood chairs of half a century earlier. Some of Dahlström's designs took functionalism in unexpected directions, for example his BD Relax chair (2000). This was an outdoor lounge chair in bent steel tube and fabric, featuring a sleeping bag for comfort in the chill of a Scandinavian evening.

At the same time as these smaller manufacturers were championing contemporary designers, the Swedish furniture retailer IKEA was transforming the international furniture market. Many of its basic products, such as the Billy bookcase, were functional design at its most elemental and inexpensive. They were utilitarian objects for the mass market. In 1995, however, IKEA entered the high-end market with a capsule collection of 40 products by 19 young Swedish designers, showing that New Functionalism was not the preserve of 'boutique' manufacturers. The collection was titled IKEA PS, acknowledging that it was an addition to the main collection, and was conceived by Lennart Ekmark, the head of IKEA's product development, brand manager Stefan Ytterborn and the designers Thomas Eriksson and Thomas Sandell. IKEA PS launched at the Milan Furniture Fair, and comprised furniture and homeware recognizable in style, if not price,

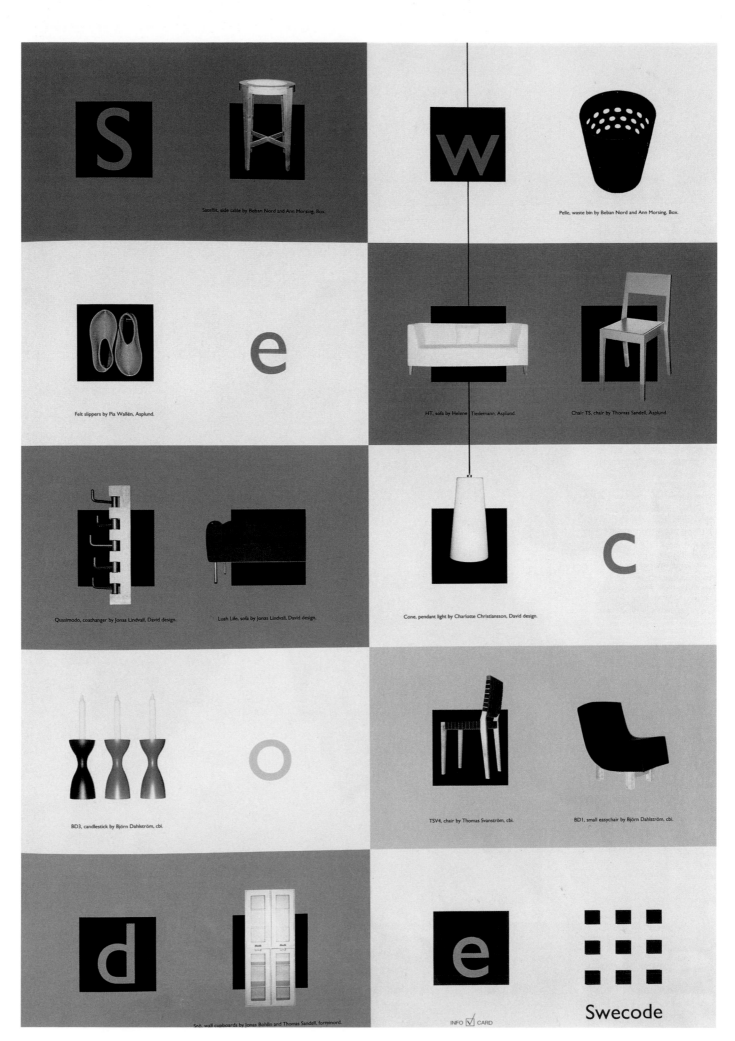

Saxellit, side table by Beban Nord and Ann Morsing, Box.

Pelle, waste bin by Beban Nord and Ann Morsing, Box.

Felt slippers by Pia Wallén, Asplund.

HT, sofa by Helene Tiedemann, Asplund.

Chair TS, chair by Thomas Sandell, Asplund.

Quasimodo, coathanger by Jonas Lindvall, David design.

Lush Life, sofa by Jonas Lindvall, David design.

Cone, pendant light by Charlotte Christiansson, David design.

BD3, candlestick by Björn Dahlström, cbi.

TSV4, chair by Thomas Svanström, cbi.

BD1, small easychair by Björn Dahlström, cbi.

Snö, wall cupboards by Jonas Bohlin and Thomas Sandell, formnord.

INFO ☑ CARD

Swecode

BD1 chair, designed by Björn
Dahlström, manufactured
by CBI, Sweden, 1994. Birch,
high density foam, cotton
upholstery. V&A: W.16-1997,
given by CBI / KLARA AB.

IKEA PS Klocka, designed by
Thomas Eriksson, manufactured
by IKEA, Sweden, 1994. Lacquered
steel and MDF. Photo: V&A.

Loop table, designed by Barber
Osgerby, manufactured by Isokon
Plus, UK, 1996. Birch plywood.
V&A: W.2-2000.

from the catalogues of David Design, Asplund
and Cappellini's Progetto Oggetto. Crucially,
IKEA could distribute the collection globally
and the objects were very affordably priced,
although relatively expensive compared to its
other ranges. In Italy high-end manufacturers
had championed New Functionalism to stave
off recession and as a stylistic break with the
1980s, but with IKEA it became mainstream.

Jasper Morrison's influence has run
like a thread through the story of New
Functionalist furniture design, but what of his
successors? Edward Barber and Jay Osgerby
are English architects and designers a decade
younger than Morrison who share a design
sensibility with him. Like Morrison, they
studied at the Royal College of Art; unlike him
they studied architecture and interior design,
graduating in 1994. As with Morrison, it is

possible to connect these designers to a tradition of modernist furniture, this time through
the conduit of Windmill Furniture, a West
London company run by Chris and Lone
McCourt. At the core of the company's output
are reissues of plywood modernist furniture
first made by Isokon, most notably the Long
Chair by Marcel Breuer of 1936. Through its
Isokon Plus brand, Windmill Furniture created a high-quality catalogue of contemporary
furniture with a number of young designers,
including Michael Sodeau and Shin and
Tomoko Azumi. After the RCA, Barber
Osgerby's first commission was for a bar interior in South Kensington, London, for which
they designed a low plywood table. The client
could not afford the table, but the designers
developed it anyway with Windmill, launching it as the Loop Table in 1996. Although
the table looked like a continuous strip of
plywood, in fact it was made of two shallow
conjoined 'U's. It was an instant media
success and in 1997 won them a coveted 'Best
New Designers' award at the International
Contemporary Furniture Fair (ICFF) in New
York. Barber Osgerby included a Loop table
on the stand they designed for *Wallpaper**
magazine at the 1997 100% Design fair,
where it was seen by Giulio Cappellini. With
Cappellini, the pair extended the design language of the table, principally derived from
radius corners, to make a family of attenuated,
elegant furniture including a desk, a bench
and a chaise longue. These were undoubtedly
designed according to functionalist principles,
but equally they represented the apogee
of late-1990s functionalist style too.[21]

'We are not "big-statement" designers,
but interested in well-resolved, simple
products with multi-layered details,' said Jay

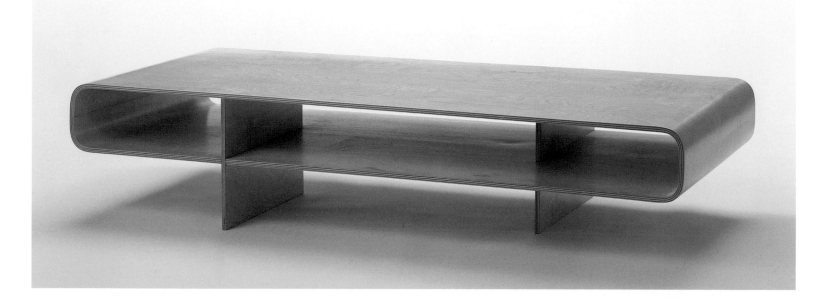

De La Warr chair, designed
by Barber Osgerby, manufactured
by Established & Sons, UK, 2006.
Computer rendering: courtesy
of Established & Sons.

Loop desk, designed by Barber
Osgerby, manufactured by
Cappellini, Italy, 1999. Birch
plywood, stainless steel, nylon.
Photo: courtesy of Barber Osgerby.

Osgerby, by which he meant he wanted his
furniture to have enduring material quality
and aesthetic appeal.[22] The constraint of
a well-defined brief helped Barber Osgerby
produce some elegant and timeless furniture,
including the choir stalls for St Thomas's
Cathedral, Portsmouth (2003), and dining
furniture for the De La Warr Pavilion in
Bexhill-on-Sea, East Sussex (2006). At
Portsmouth the brief was for a bench made
of an enduring material that could be used
by three choirboys but moved by one. The
result features the characteristic radius curves
of their other work, but also has a reserve
associated with a previous generation
of English furniture designers such as Luke
Hughes and Ron Carter. At Bexhill, the challenge was to respond to Erich Mendelsohn's
iconic modernist building without aping
the architecture or the Alvar Aalto furniture
that originally filled it. The simplicity, even
austerity, of Barber Osgerby's furniture, made
by Established & Sons, complemented and
enhanced the interiors of Britain's most
important modernist building.

For Edward Barber and Jay Osgerby,
functionalism is neither a conceptual stance
nor a political gesture. Their design is continuous with a modest English tradition, rooted

in the Arts and Crafts ethic of a designer such as Gordon Russell, favouring thoughtfulness and humility over displays of passion or excess. They have sometimes been decorative, as with their interiors for Stella McCartney's boutiques (constructed for them by Cappellini), but more usually functionalist; design is about problem-solving, not expressing personality traits, and by nature they are unassuming. Simon Pengelly is another extremely modest designer who can claim more products in production than most of his peers. In the 1990s he designed much of the furniture for Habitat, and more recently he has supported small independent British manufacturers, such as Modus and Hitch Mylius, who produce functionalist modern furniture, often for the contract market. This is good modern furniture but not leading-edge design.

Shin and Tomoko Azumi are Japanese designers who have lived in London since 1992 when they arrived as students. After graduation from the RCA they founded Azumi in 1995 and until 2005 their work was all co-signed: subsequently they designed independently. Azumi and Barber Osgerby share a palette and repertoire of materials, a similarity not overlooked by the organizers of the 2004 Jerwood Prize exhibition where the two teams were presented opposite one another across the gallery in a face-off of pared-back plywood functionalism (Barber Osgerby won).[23] Inspired by their upbringing in Japan, where homes are often small and furniture is movable and light-weight, Azumi designed several pieces that transform from one function to another. Evoking the theme of anonymity that has pervaded this chapter, Tomoko Azumi once said, 'I want to make furniture that was light and airy, not chunky volumes in small spaces but pieces that disappear in space.'[24] The Azumis were interested in maximizing the function of furniture, not exploring its symbolism. The best-known example was Table=Chest (which was actually Tomoko's RCA degree piece in 1995) that transformed from a chest of drawers to a low table. Other self-explanatory pieces included Bench=Bed (1996) and Armchair=Table (1997). Although these objects were widely published and exhibited, they never achieved the mass production that the designers desired. In the case of the Table=Chest, the angled joints proved prohibitively expensive.[25] Azumi achieved commercial success with designs for La Palma, an Italian manufacturer of plywood furniture, with whom they collaborated since 1997. These pieces were not transformable,

Stripey cabinet, designed
by Simon Pengelly, manufactured
by Modus, UK, 2003. Lacquered
MDF, oak, brushed stainless
steel. Photo: courtesy of Modus.

but shared lightness and usefulness with their foldable cousins, and many of them were designed to stack. They also designed objects for the Japanese homeware store Muji, which has popularized minimal design since its arrival in Britain in 1991. The Orbital workstation for schools was a radical design and featured a swivel seat attached to a circular desk, allowing greater flexibility of classroom layouts. It was part of the Design Council's Furniture for the Future project in 2003 and was developed for manufacture by the Keen Group Ltd.

New Functionalism was a response to the 'design of excess' that became associated with the 1980s. It helped to move forward design debates that seemed to have grounded on postmodernism. Moreover, New Functionalism represented designers' and manufacturers' quest for sobriety in a period of economic boom and bust. Functionalism and minimalism swept furniture design clean in the early and mid-1990s, but because this was a reductive design process, inevitably it ran the risk of running itself into a cul-de-sac. By the turn of the millennium a new strain of design had emerged, based on fun, not function.

Table=Chest, designed by Tomoko Azumi, made by Frank E. Bailey, UK, 1995. Beech, beech veneered MDF. V&A: W.6-1997.

Jasper Morrison

Plywood chair, manufactured
by Vitra, 1994. Birch plywood.
V&A: W.1-1995, given
by Vitra Ltd.

Exploded diagram of Plywood
chair, drawing by Jasper
Morrison, 1988. Courtesy
of Jasper Morrison.

Bottlerack, manufactured
by Magis, Italy, polypropylene
and anodized aluminium, 1994.
Photo: Miro Zagnoli / Magis.

'I like ideas like normal, soft, comfortable, easy to use. Don't forget that people have to live with the objects we design. We need to understand how they can be used and think about everyday life. Design is something real.' [1]

He may be a designer who has defined an era, but there is something very down-to-earth about Jasper Morrison. He wants to design objects of such plainness they are almost invisible. One way he did this was to take existing forms and reuse them. The leg of one of his Cappellini sofas was basically an upturned dumb-bell; his door handles for FSB were shaped like light bulbs and taxi door handles. This approach is not strictly speaking recycling, nor is it minimalism, but it acknowledges that there are already near-perfect forms that need no adjustment. The designer's task is to reconfigure this vocabulary of forms.

Morrison admitted his admiration for children's cartoons whose visual style was a 'kind of distillation of objects into almost ridiculous simplicity.' [2] He appreciated that simplification made the cartoon characters more expressive, not less, because anything extraneous was discarded. Some of Morrison's designs have a similar graphic quality (the critic Peter Dormer called it 'typographic' [3]). Morrison describes it as 'a kind of play-off of 2-D and 3-D. Lines seen from different angles, lines that describe a volume rather than creating one.' [4] As a result, throughout his 20-year career much of his work has seemed almost two-dimensional in its simplicity.

This is certainly true of the installations for Vitra that made his name at the end of the 1980s. Titled 'Some new items for the home', the installations looked like a living room, but the chairs, tables, rugs and bottles all seemed to be acting the part of real objects, like stage props. His plywood chairs were almost like diagrams of themselves and there is a constant tension between the archetype and the actual in his work.

Morrison has enjoyed productive and lasting relationships with manufacturers, notably SCP, Vitra and Cappellini, dating back to the 1980s. In 1997, however, he designed his largest product to date, a tram for the city of Hanover. In many ways Morrison can be described as the natural heir of Dieter Rams, whose designs for Braun exemplified post-war German industrial design principles, based on logic and clarity. Also in the late 1990s Morrison embarked on a successful collaboration with the Italian manufacturer Magis, designing plastic furniture for a scale of mass-production he had not achieved before. The most notable outcome of this partnership was the Air range of chairs and tables (see page 92).

Some new items for the home, Part II, installation by Jasper Morrison for Vitra at Gallery Fac-Simile, Milan, 1989. Photo: Morrison Studio, London.

Konstantin Grcic

'He's a designer who's not out to change the world, yet he creates objects that suggest types of behaviour, and pursues demanding, neutral, well-thought-out projects that are bound to have a lasting effect.'[1]

Achille Castiglioni regarded Konstantin Grcic as the best designer of the younger generation, and in response Grcic admitted that a 1984 catalogue of Castiglioni's work inspired his career choice: 'It's his fault I became a designer!'[2] Both are cerebral designers who create furniture and objects that are fit for their purpose, over and above being essays in style or fashion.

Konstantin Grcic was born in 1965 in Munich and now has his studio there. Unusually for an industrial designer, he trained as a craftsman in wood, at the influential but now defunct Parnham College in Dorset run by John Makepeace. Making his own furniture helped him to understand appropriate materials and methods for industrially manufactured objects, but he has long ceased to make his own designs himself. A typical Grcic design will appear to be simple and straightforward at first glance, but on closer inspection it will reveal nuances and subtleties. The Mayday light for Flos, for example, was a plastic cone on

a wire like an industrial work light. 'You can hang it up, lie it on the floor, kick it' he said. 'I always have lamps knocking around my office and home, but I could never be bothered to fix one in the ceiling.'[3] Like the designer, it is unpretentious but not simplistic.

In 1990 Konstantin Grcic graduated from the Royal College of Art and for a time he worked in Jasper Morrison's studio. This placed him at the centre of the New Functionalist group of designers associated with Morrison, James Irvine and the manufacturers SCP and Cappellini. The following year saw Grcic's return to Munich to set up on his own. His early furniture tended to be made in timber and metal, such as the Refolo all-metal trolley he designed for Driade to house computers, stereos or televisions (1995). The design was strictly functional, but escaped the aesthetic of the office by featuring strong colours for the different clip-on elements. Its flexibility and suitability to the home-office reflected trends in domestic design at the time. Humble plastic products such as laundry baskets and waste-paper bins for the German manufacturer Authentics opened the mass-market to his designs.

Grcic developed the Chair One range (2001–4) with Magis in Italy, a company more generally known for its plastic objects and furniture.[4] Chair One was a linear triangulated metal grid, cast in aluminium, that was a development away from the curved geometries of his earlier New Functionalist designs and towards a new aesthetic of crystals and fractals. His Miura stool for Plank in 2005 was even simpler and strikingly sculptural. 'The beauty of products we are talking about lies in their simplicity. So, the question is rather how to make them more simple than making them more complex. I am critical towards the idea of over-engineering. I would like to think there is a certain appropriateness of means and economy.'[5]

Miura bar stool, manufactured by Plank, Italy, 2005. Polypropylene. Photo: courtesy of Plank.

Chair One; manufactured by
Magis, Italy, 2004, die-cast
aluminium, polyester coating.
Photo: Carlo Lavatori.

Osorom seating unit,
manufactured by Moroso,
Italy, 2005, fibreglass and
resin. Photo: Courtesy
of KGID.

Cy-borg sideboard, designed
by Nick Dine, manufactured by
Dune, USA, 2003. Birch plywood,
MDF, polyurethane. Photo:
courtesy of Dune.

Chapter Three

Neo-Pop

'When I first saw 2001,
I didn't know who Stanley
Kubrick was, or what it was
about, but it totally blew me
away. I loved it and wanted
to be in an environment
just like it. Every detail
was perfect.'

'What I really liked about
1950s, 1960s and 1970s design
was the modernity. Now it's
increasingly difficult to design
something truly modern.' [1]

Marc Newson

New Functionalism was one way designers and manufacturers tried to cope with the hangover of Memphis. But for many, New Functionalism was merely warmed-up modernism, complete with all the moralizing, dogma and utopianism of its 1920s antecedent. Instead, designers sought a different type of modernity that was less puritan and reductive, more commercial, more populist and more fun. Like Marc Newson, some of them found inspiration in the design of the space-race era, and in movies such as 2001, *A Space Odyssey* (1968), which envisioned a kind of seamless modernism of science fiction, pods and new synthetic materials. Other designers looked at cartoon books and their weird characters. The organic design of optimistic mid-twentieth-century modernism was revived, both as reissues of classics by the Eameses, Saarinen, Bertoia and Panton, and in new furniture. This reflexive process of looking back at how the past predicted the future has been termed 'Retro-Futurism'. Canadian furniture and product designer Karim Rashid succinctly calls it 'Futuretro', but here I shall refer to it as 'neo-Pop', because it was inspired by that previous era's popular fantasy of futuristic design.

Rashid is one of the most visible neo-Pop designers, and its greatest apologist. Writing in 2003, Rashid noted that although the 1990s rejected postmodernism, design in the new century plunders the past even more than during the 1980s, and he asked why. 'Is it that the yuppies and the boomers currently empowered in the market are trying to revisit their past, and are not willing to let go? Is it a fear of mortality? Maybe we collectively see the past as more interesting than now and so we copy it without compunction, consciously or subconsciously.' He admitted that we are drawn to the past because technological

breakthroughs mean 'now we can make the past better', especially the kind of 'seamless techno-organic world' that was imagined in the 1960s. But Rashid knows retrospection can be lazy, since 'it is easier to simulate the past than predict the future'.[2]

Why did mid-century modernism and the Pop design of the 1960s become popular references for the 1990s? An initial reason was that a critical distance emerged between the past and the present that enabled a new generation to discover historic design. Comprehensive exhibitions such as 'Les Années Pop' at the Centre Pompidou in 2001 reassessed the art and architecture of the period, providing a context for a reappraisal of furniture design. Designers such as Charles and Ray Eames, Verner Panton and Joe Colombo were reconsidered both critically and in the market-place. As explored in the Introduction, the market for twentieth-century design classics expanded greatly during the 1990s, not only encouraging a connoisseurship of original mid-century pieces, but also the reissue of very many influential designs. These in turn inspired designers to create new works that were, to a lesser or greater degree, look-alikes. For example, the organically shaped one-piece plywood seat and back of chairs by Arne Jacobsen, and the fibreglass or plastic chairs by the Eameses or Robin Day, were clearly influences on 1990s chairs by, amongst others, Christophe Pillet and Ross Lovegrove. In 1969 Verner Panton designed the Pantower, a vertical upholstered monolith with an organic cut-out centre into which the sitter clambered, which was closer to being an architectural structure than it was to a chair. The Pantower was reprised by the Vitra Design Museum in 1999, by which time it had spawned a look-alike, the Passepartout by Giovanni Lauda and Dante Donegani for

Magazine sofa, designed by
Michael Young, manufactured
by twentytwentyone, UK, 1995.
Plywood and solid beech structure,
stainless steel legs, polyurethane
foam, wool upholstery. Photo:
courtesy of twentytwentyone.

Edra in 1998.[3] Fabio Novembre's 'And' combinable seating for Cappellini (2001) also paid homage to the Pantower, though less overtly. Like Passepartout, it enveloped the sitter in a miniature upholstered architectural framework, apparently inspired by a string of DNA molecules, recreating for the present the essence of Panton's 1960s 'total environments'.

The rounded rectangle, or radius corner, was adopted by designers *en masse* in the 1990s to signify 1960s and 1970s Pop modernity, not just in furniture but notably in graphics as well. Because it could be produced so easily across materials and techniques, in two and three dimensions, from about 1995 it was one of the most overused devices for furniture, rapidly becoming a shorthand for design of the period. The curves were geometric yet sensuous and can be regarded as the antithesis of the hard right angles that typified minimalist furniture. Boxes became less box-like. Curved corners softened and humanized

contemporary design, and coupled with shiny lacquer surfaces in bright colours, they made functional furniture more fun and less severe.

For the same reasons the radius curve had been used in some 1960s furniture, such as Anna Castelli Ferrieri's Multi-Box storage system for Kartell (1968), but not as much as in furniture a quarter of a century later (bearing out Karim Rashid's assertion that, more than ever, the past is plundered today). Marc Newson and Michael Young were early adopters, and like Ronan and Erwan Bouroullec they made the radius corner part of their personal design signatures. It appears throughout their oeuvres, often combined with a hollow interior, as in Young's Magazine sofa (1995). Barber Osgerby used it for the Loop range in 1996 but, made of plywood, it results from the material and technology rather than from applied Pop aesthetics. The radius corners of Nick Dine's Cy-borg sideboard (2003), however, did not derive

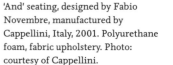

'And' seating, designed by Fabio Novembre, manufactured by Cappellini, Italy, 2001. Polyurethane foam, fabric upholstery. Photo: courtesy of Cappellini.

from technology but were deliberate notes of Pop styling. Storage systems or towers combining differently sized radius-cornered containers were designed by Lloyd Schwan in New York and the Czech design studio Olgoj Chorchoj.[4] The radius corner was truly international, appearing in furniture ranges from Sweden (Box Design), the US (Dune), Italy (Cappellini), Turkey (Derin) and just about everywhere else. It is such an easy device to replicate that it became the staple signifier of modernity used by every young designer (and also the means by which they hoped to emulate the success of designers such as Newson). Its use was allied to the rise of computer-aided design as early digital graphics programmes lent themselves to the endless repetition of simple geometric forms. As the software developed, more sophisticated, biomorphic shapes could be achieved on screen.

Michael Young and the Bouroullec brothers design similar furniture and objects. Perhaps this is because both Young and the Bouroullecs design three-dimensional objects that have the character of two-dimensional graphics, often rendered in seamless materials such as corian or plastic, and often with monochrome or white surfaces. These designers produce relatively rarefied, purist products for the same top-end manufacturers (for example, Cappellini). Their geometric, shiny furniture is Retro-Futurist, and merges furniture with lighting and architecture. Young's Sticklight (1999) and the Bouroullecs' Objet Lumineux (1998) were both big lamps that were symmetrical white, glowing poles, swelling and tapering along their length. Young's furniture tended to be humorous and cartoon-like. A brief from Magis was for furniture that would put a smile on your face; Young duly designed low seats called Yogi, after the cartoon bear (2002). The Bouroullecs' furniture is more akin to the futuristic world encountered by Monsieur Hulot in *Mon Oncle* (1958). Together they became part of an international young design elite, typified by Michael Young's own Reykjavik-based jewellery brand, Smak, which marketed objects by the Bouroullecs, Michael Marriott, Matali Crasset, Richard Hutten and Ineke Hans.

Tom Dixon was Michael Young's mentor in the early 1990s when Young was still a student at Kingston University. Young worked in Dixon's studio, Space, and admired his scrap-metal furniture, although he never pursued salvage in his own work. By the mid-1990s Dixon was developing a Pop aesthetic more akin to Verner Panton's plastic,

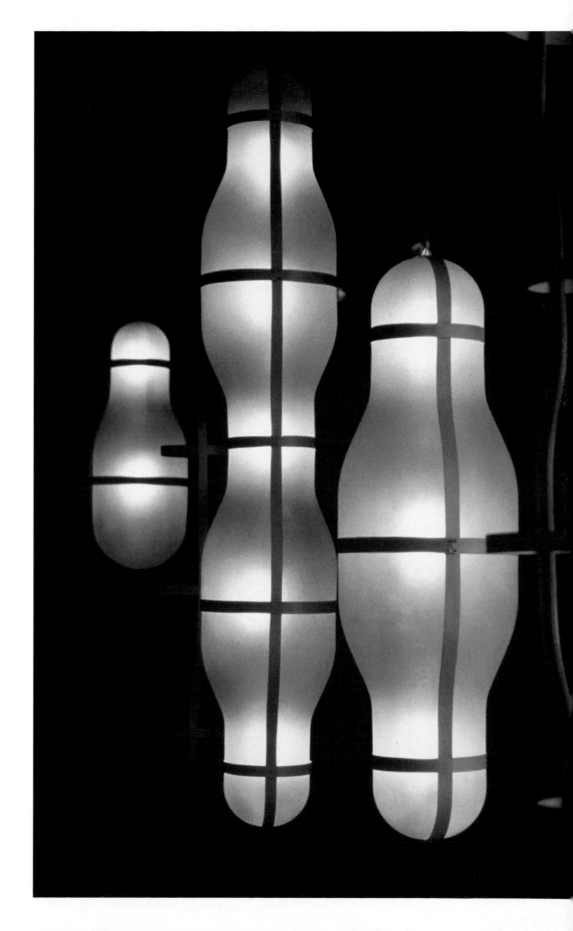

Objets Lumineux, designed by Ronan and Erwan Bouroullec, manufactured by Cappellini, 1998 1999. Birch plywood, thermoform Altuglass®. Photo: Morgane Le Gall.

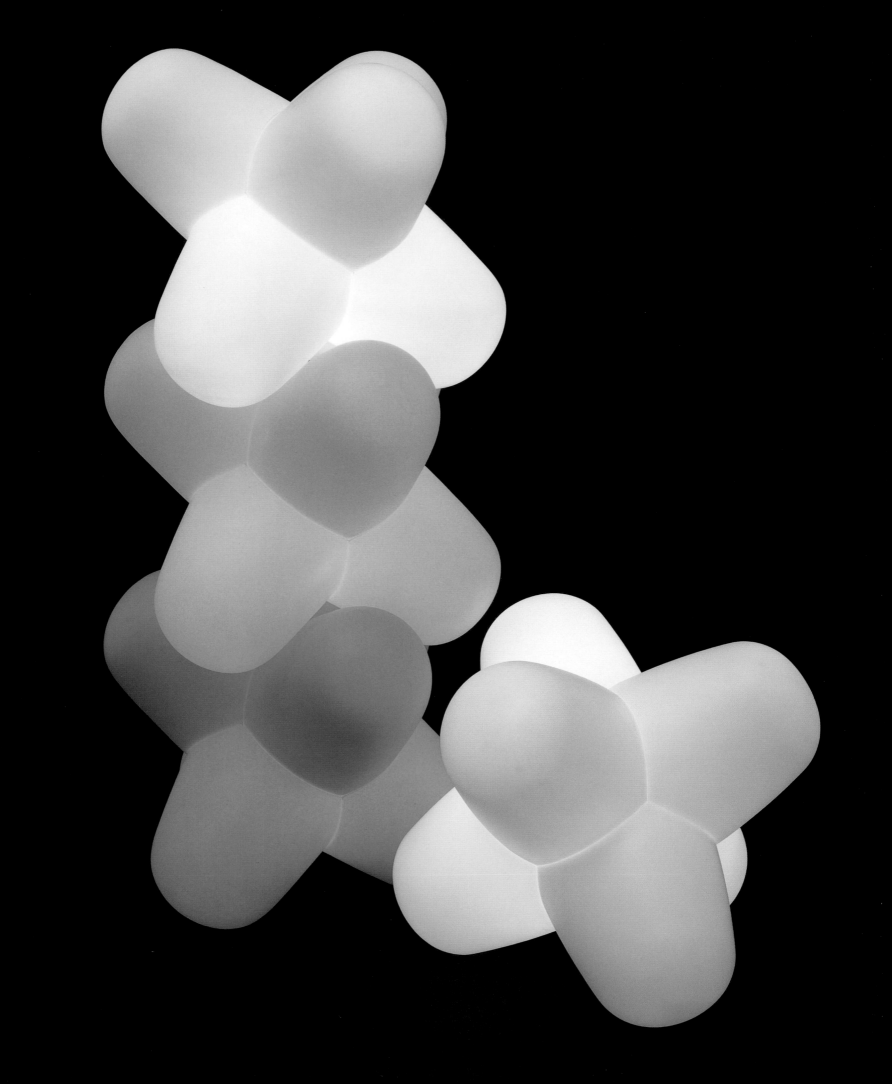

Jacklights, designed by
Tom Dixon, manufactured
by Eurolounge, UK, 1996.
Rotation-moulded polyethylene.
V&A: W.8to11-1997.

Dog House kennel, designed
by Michael Young, manufactured
by Magis, Italy, 2001. Rotation-
moulded polyethylene, steel
rod. Photo: Giancarlo Maiocchi.

geometric nightclub look, typified by the Jacklight (1996), a durable, stackable, rotation-moulded five-pointed star that could be a stool or a lamp. The Jacklight was his first product to approach mass production and marked a turning-point in Dixon's career. In 1994 Michael Young formed his own studio to design highly recognizable, media-friendly furniture in a deliberate bid to launch himself internationally. 'I realized that to get noticed by industry I would have to design in a noticeable way,' he recalled.[5] Like Marc Newson, Michael Young was able to capitalize on manufacturers' new love affair with designers, a relationship brokered by Philippe Starck in the 1980s. Starck's success in the media and at the cash register led many companies to seek other 'mediagenic' designers.[6] Young's furniture, therefore, was intended to seduce, not shock, and within several years designs such as the Magazine sofa and the Smartie pouf had made him a design star in Britain, Japan and Italy. For Sawaya & Moroni in Milan Young designed simplified comma-like timber seats that owed little to traditional chair-making and nothing to ergonomics. A white set was included in a joint exhibition with Jasper Morrison and Marc Newson in Reykjavik, Young's adopted home, in 1999.[7] In the early 2000s Young moved into a more accessible market with many designs for the

Italian plastics specialist Magis, all of which share wit and simplicity, and elicit direct emotional responses from their target consumers (the Dog House kennel, for example).

A design for a Disintegrated Kitchen (effectively, a modular kitchen system) by Ronan Bouroullec was spotted by Giulio Cappellini at the Paris Salon du Meuble in January 1998. Cappellini reserved great praise for the young Frenchman, describing him as 'exactly like his designs: light, discreet, ironic, professional'[8]. The Cappellini commissions were more than Ronan could manage alone, so from 1999 he collaborated with his brother Erwan. Hole was a series of tables and consoles deriving entirely from radius-curved plywood in-filled with glass. The one-legged Hole console (1999) was even simpler than Jasper Morrison's one-legged table, also for Cappellini (1986). The Glide sofa in 2001 had a familial likeness to the Eameses' Aluminium Group and Soft Pad chairs (1958 and 1969, respectively), via Morrison's Low Pad chairs (1999). All shared weightless upholstered shells on skinny metal frames: the Bouroullecs incorporated a shelf and a chaise into their sofa so that it became like a miniature contraction of the living room itself. Erwan Bouroullec's Lit Clos (2000) also merged architecture and furniture, like the best Pop designs. It was a bed in a box, raised on stilts like a room within

Brick module, designed by
Ronan and Erwan Bouroullec,
manufactured in polystyrene
by Gallery Kreo, Paris,
2000; manufactured in wood
by Cappellini, Italy, 2001.
Photo: Morgane Le Gall.

Lit Clos bed, designed by Erwan
Bouroullec, edition of 12 for Gallery
Kreo, Paris, 2000. Painted birch
plywood, steel, aluminium,
thermoform Altuglass®, fabric.
Photo: Morgane Le Gall.

Rainbow chair, designed by
Patrick Norguet, manufactured
by Cappellini, Italy, 2000.
Acrylic sheets bonded by
ultrasound. Photo: courtesy
of Cappellini.

a room. Their Brick (2000) and Cloud (2002) polystyrene modules were hybrid screens, shelves and room dividers, but principally neo-Pop theatrical dressing. The aluminium Hole chair (2000) was painted lurid green with a *trompe-l'oeil* vertical stripe that made it look iridescent. Fellow French designer Patrick Norguet's acrylic Rainbow chair in the same year was the star of Cappellini's show and really did shine with vertical candy stripes.

To an extent, this view of both Young and the Bouroullecs over-emphasizes their dependence on Retro-Futurist motifs, and downplays their ability to design functionally. Yet it is fair to say their design depends on the seduction of forms, volumes and surfaces, often recalling earlier essays in futuristic design, rather than revealed structures and craftsmanship. As such it typified fashionable neo-Pop furniture design since 1990.

A potent influence on many designers was Ken Adam's designs for futuristic fantasy films. *Dr Strangelove* and *Goldfinger* (both 1964), *You Only Live Twice* (1967) and *Diamonds Are Forever* (1971) certainly influenced the design of the Austin Powers parodies (1997, 1999, 2002), which were also enthused with a nostalgia for 'Swinging London', a nostalgia that was evoked by the new Labour government's attempt to rebrand Britain through design after its 1997 election victory. The young design company Inflate represented this new spirit in 1990s British design that was saturated in a Pop sensibility. Led by Nick Crosbie, Inflate set out to make 'fun, functional and affordable' products, at first made from inflated PVC, later from dip-moulded PVC and then from more diverse processes. The use of plastics and inflatables, plus the acid palette, relate these objects to 1960s design. It is easy to evoke another seminal 1960s futuristic movie here, too: *Barbarella*, designed by Mario Garbuglia in 1968 (the fashion-futurist Paco Rabanne designed Jane Fonda's costumes). In the movie, the interior of Barbarella's space ship is an inflatable, and blow-up design was at its most fashionable in the late 1960s. Collaborations with designers including Michael Young and Michael Marriott earn Inflate an important position in 1990s British design, and in the appeal of neo-Pop design internationally.[9] *Barbarella* also inspired Ross Lovegrove's sofa of the same name for Moooi in 2005; he imagined 'making love with an amazing blond like Barbarella' on its shaggy sheepskin cover.[10]

2001, A Space Odyssey, directed
by Stanley Kubrick, 1968, featuring
Djinn chairs, designed by Olivier
Mourgue, 1963, manufactured
by Airborne, France, 1964.
Photo: BFI Stills.

Neo-Pop design was about optimism and utopianism, symbolized by the seamless, curved, pod shapes of the interiors and furniture in these fantasy and science-fiction films. Marc Newson was powerfully influenced by the same films, and reserved particular praise for Stanley Kubrick's *2001, A Space Odyssey*. Olivier Mourgue's Djinn chairs (1963) contributed greatly to the look and feel of *2001*, but Newson's own chairs, such as the Embryo (1988), would have fitted equally well. The Pod Bar he designed in Tokyo's fashionable Roppongi district in 1989 was a homage to *2001*, as was the Skoda boutique in Berlin in 1992, which featured Embryo chairs.[11] Newson's Retro-Futurism suited the optimistic, youthful and glamorous world of upmarket fashion stores, bars and restaurants that he designed in world cities such as London, New York and Tokyo.

Another way that Pop design was differentiated from functionalism was through luxury. Pop products are not ascetic; there is no moral imperative for them to be reductive. This is certainly true of most furniture by the Italian manufacturer Edra, founded in 1987 by Valerio Mazzei with Massimo Morozzi as art director. In 1966 Morozzi had formed Archizoom Associati with Andrea Branzi, Gilberto Corretti and Paolo Deganello (disbanded in 1974). The members of Archizoom were interested in technological utopias, kitsch and Surrealism, and designed radical furniture such as a conversation pit upholstered in faux leopard skin (the Safari seating unit for Poltronova, 1967) that stimulated more debate than sales.[12] The group even participated in 'The New Domestic Landscape' exhibition at MOMA, New York, in 1972. Edra, therefore, is a direct descendant of high-style Italian experimentation from the Pop era and makes extravagant, expensive and excessive furniture for the highest end of the

market. Edra furniture has been likened to haute couture in the world of fashion. It is luxury unbounded. It also recalls the 'total environments' of Pop design, where furniture and architecture elided. The Meditation Pod (2001) by Steven Blaess was an upholstered dish, shaped like a clover leaf, inside which the user could curl. Pods are like rooms-within-rooms and were frequent references in 1960s Pop design. The Boa sofa (2002) by the Brazilian brothers Fernando and Humberto Campana was just 90 metres (300ft) of structureless polyurethane-filled velvet tube, knotted into a nest over 3 metres (10ft) long. The sensuous (and sensual) velvet rolls engulfed the sprawled users, who could not sit decorously on the Boa if they tried. It was another kind of micro-architecture, if not exactly a pod.

Unencumbered by cost considerations, Edra furniture also featured innovative materials, often fabrics, and advanced mechanics that enabled nine separate elements of Francesco Binfaré's Flap sofa (2000) to raise independently, like fronds on a fern. Reaching a degree of luxury unsurpassed in recent furniture design history, Edra spangled a Flap sofa with 750,000 crystals in 2001 (see page 139). The Diamond sofa was a glamorous collaboration with Swarovski that brought furniture and fashion design together in a relationship explored in greater depth in Chapter Six.

Edra supplies luxurious, sometimes experimental furniture to an elite market, but most neo-Pop objects are intended to compete in an increasingly saturated mass market. Manufacturers and designers have sought new ways to differentiate their products and attract customers. 'Almost all the functional problems had already found a solution, we are working much more on expression', recalled Alberto Alessi whose family firm became the benchmark for 'added-value by design'.[13] Expressive, characterful, anthropomorphic tableware designed by great architects and avant-garde designers made Alessi a leading, and much emulated, design force in the 1990s. Even though Starck denied that rocket imagery equated with modernity, his Juicy Salif lemon squeezer for Alessi (1990) was pure 'Buck Rogers'. Starck reworked the language of science-fiction fantasy: his first company was named after a Philip K. Dick novel and many of his products take their names from the author's characters. Many Alessi products, by Starck, Giovannoni and others, were 'cutensils', a contraction of 'cute utensils', styled like little cartoon characters to make

Boa sofa, designed by Fernando
and Humberto Campana,
manufactured by Edra, Italy,
2002. Velvet tube filled with
polyurethane foam chips.
Photo: courtesy of Edra.

Bombo bar stools, designed
by Stefano Giovannoni, manufactured
by Magis, Italy, 1997. Chromed
steel, injection-moulded ABS.
Photo: courtesy of Magis.

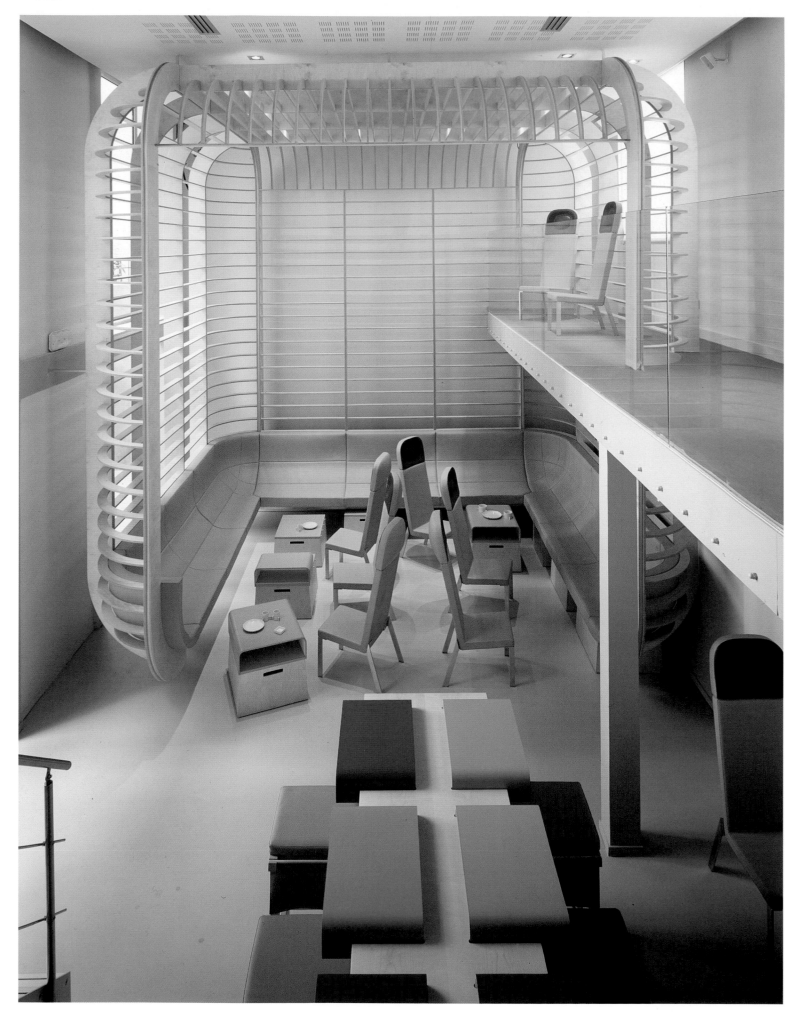

The bar of the Hi Hotel, Nice,
designed by Matali Crasset, 2003,
including Capuche chairs from
the Domodinamica collection
manufactured by Modular S.r.L.,
Italy. Photo: Uwe Spoering.

Morfeo sofa-bed, designed by
Stefano Giovannoni and Rodrigo
Torres, Domodinamica collection
manufactured by Modular S.r.L.,
Italy, 2004. Polyurethane foam,
elastic upholstery, adjustable
electric light fittings. Photo:
courtesy of Modular S.r.L.

them more appealing and stimulate sales.[14]

A group of designers, including Stefano Giovannoni and Massimo Iosa Ghini, grew out of Memphis in the late 1980s and called themselves the 'Bolidismo', a term loaded with the dangerous speed and dynamism of meteors. Iosa Ghini had been a successful comic-book illustrator and his furniture was imbued with the spirit of the golden age of comic-strip heroes. The Bolidismo were careening into the future, but through their objects it looked like the future imagined for Dan Dare in the 1950s, Buck Rogers in the 1930s, or further back, like Marinetti's Futurist visions in the 1920s. Of all the Bolidismo group, Stefano Giovannoni enjoyed the most success, designing a variety of objects across media that were unified by their bubble-like character. Commercially the most successful is the Bombo family of seating and tables for Magis (introduced in 1997); 300,000 Bombo bar stools have been sold, and fakes and look-alikes have appeared on the market made by other companies attempting to profit from its popularity. The droplet shape that characterizes the range of bar stools, chairs and tables, in injection-moulded ABS, polycarbonate or die-cast aluminium, is another design trope that frequently reoccurred in neo-Pop design.

The Italian manufacturer Modular, founded in 1973, made some of the most cartoon-like furniture of the 1990s under its Domodinamica brand, acquired in 1996. Playfulness and child-like innocence go hand-in-hand with this neo-Pop design. Denis Santachiara contributed Cicalino Ecologico (1989), a kitsch doormat complete with a cartoon-like plastic bird on a stem that sang when the mat was trodden on. His bubble-shaped Swing armchair and sofa (1996), though large, unusually were also rockers. Modular manufactured the Capuche chair designed by Santachiara's former associate, the French designer Matali Crasset, in 2000 and used by her in the interiors of the Hi Hotel in Nice. Much of her work is concerned with child-like play and the imagination, and this furniture collection had the quality of children's building blocks in soft colours. Stefano Giovannoni and Rodrigo Torres added an extraordinary sofabed to the Domodinamica range in 2004. Named after Morfeo, the god of dreams and sleep, it shared more in common with Shrek, the computer-generated ogre of several successful movies, mostly due to its luminous green upholstery and movable trumpet-like lamps that were suggestive of Shrek's ears.

Morfeo was definitely a friendly design, soft, engulfing and cheerful, but it was not the only piece of furniture to assume a cartoon character. Starck transformed garden gnomes into utterly kitsch tables and stools for Kartell (2000), which seem to 'snicker along with the designer at the modernist canon of functionalism'.[15] Berlin-based designer Jerszy Seymour's Muff Daddy chair for Covo in Italy (2002) was like an oversized stuffed toy with long fabric arms the sitter could wrap around themselves. Seymour's Pop references tend to come from the street and skate culture and

Alessandra armchair, designed by Javier Mariscal, manufactured by Moroso, Italy, 1995. Steel frame, polyurethane and polyester padding, wool upholstery, chromed steel legs. Photo: courtesy of Moroso.

Attila, Saint-Esprit and Napoleon stool-tables, designed by Philippe Starck, manufactured by Kartell, Italy, 2000. Thermoplastic technopolymer. Photo: courtesy of Kartell.

even his logo is like a graffiti-artist's tag.[16] Similarly, Matali Crasset has branded herself with a cartoon-like smiley portrait. The Spanish graphic designer Javier Mariscal is best known for Cobi the dog, his cartoon mascot for the 1992 Barcelona Olympics, but he has also designed furniture, rugs and products for Memphis, Moroso and Alessi, amongst others. The Alessandra armchair and Saula Marina sofa he designed for Moroso in 1995 were asymmetric, curvy and comfy, upholstered in irregular patchworks that emphasized their blobby forms. Much of the appeal of this furniture was reliant on the infantilizing effect of cute and cuddly characters, a ploy borrowed by furniture designers from Manga comics.

'Blobjects' is the ugly but accurate collective term coined for a type of recent design that was curvaceous, organic, molten and bubble-like. Blobjects were popular because they were characterful, sometimes humorous and non-threatening, and always seemed more akin to nature than to technology. They had 'a pleasing plasticity of fluid *form*, a delicious sense of *color*, a chance to exist at any *scale*, a heightened sense of flowing *materiality*, and a powerful connection of our *emotions*, including a strong optimistic tendency.'[17] Although not necessarily zoomorphic, they shared traits with some of the cartoonish designs discussed

above. Blobjects were the nemesis of New Functional designs. They were all about curved surfaces and volume, and nothing to do with flat planes or structures.

Almost inevitably we find Philippe Starck was amongst the first to make blobs into furniture. In his book *Blobjects & Beyond*, Steven Skov Holt cheekily noted that 'Starck himself is a pear-shaped man with rounded-off features and an upbeat, optimistic aura. The designer of blobjects is none other than a blobject himself!'[18] In 1990 Starck designed an office for Wim Wenders, the German film director, that included a three-legged stool-cum-rest. The WW stool recalled the feelers of insects, a vegetable's new shoots, undersea cephalopods, or aliens from deep space. Later, his Os shelving had vertebra-like twisted ceramic uprights, like enormous archaeological discoveries (1998; '*os*' is French for 'bone'). Starck's blobs could be ambiguous at best, but tended to be somewhat sinister.

Like most design innovations Blobjects had precursors, such as furniture by Frederick Kiesler and Eva Zeisel's tableware, both from the 1940s.[19] Mid-century biomorphic designs derived from abstracted nature, and were the softly curved, acceptable and often commercial face of avant-garde modernism, particularly in the United States. As a teenager in Tel Aviv, Ron Arad loved 1960s Pop culture, notably

the radicalism of Bob Dylan, Robert
Rauschenberg and Claes Oldenburg (whose
sculptures were often quite blobby), and
seeing films such as *Blow Up* (1966) made
him decide to move to London.[20] Around 1992
Arad made several chairs that shared Kiesler's
amoebic forms, with flat sides held parallel by
a continuous ribbon-like surface. They were
first shown at an exhibition called 'Breeding
in Captivity', suggesting that Arad appreciated
the non-specific zoomorphism of these
objects. The critic Peter Popham described
one piece, 'Up Like A Bear', as 'a primitive
form of marine life; it just sits there, happy in
its innocent pointlessness. But it so happens
that its contours will accommodate the human
form. And people *will* keep on coming along
and dumping themselves on it. It makes the
people look ridiculous; it makes the chair look
ridiculous. But that's what keeps on happen-
ing.'[21] Kiesler worked in wood and Arad
used sheet metal and sometimes flexible
woven polished stainless steel, but as Popham
observed, even steel blobs are approachable
and fun. Arad described one of these chairs,
Creature Comfort, as a 'volume structure that
works as a chair in any position. It has no cor-
rect or incorrect way', exactly like the objects
designed by Kiesler half a century earlier.[22]
In 1992 Arad was exploring the material
qualities of steel worked by hand and had not
yet begun exploring computer-aided design.
It is ironic (or prescient), therefore, that many
of his most famous designs in highly polished
stainless steel, worked entirely by hand, had
the perfection of computer drawings, an effect
that is doubly true when they are reproduced
as photographs. The mirrored surfaces simul-
taneously described the objects as pure volumes, and dematerialized them. They were
like molten metal, and also like optical illu-
sions created on screen. Curves and bulges
characterized many neo-Pop designs, and
were Arad's signature style too.[23] In many
ways Arad's mid-'90s Blobjects – not a
term he would use himself – heralded all
the curvy, comfy, bubble-like furniture that
was to dominate at the end of the decade
and into the next century.

The Iraqi-born architect Zaha Hadid
entered the Architectural Association school
in 1972, the year before Arad. Initially Ron
Arad made furniture because it was so difficult
for young architects to build, a frustration
shared by Hadid. Since 2000 she has designed
several seating collections with the Italian
manufacturers Sawaya & Moroni that explored
her architectural ideas in miniature (their
collaboration originated with a tea and coffee

WW stool, designed by Philippe
Starck, manufactured by Vitra,
Germany, 1990. Sand-blasted
lacquered aluminium. Photo:
Hans Hansen.

D Sofa, designed by Ron Arad, edition of 20 made by One Off Ltd, UK, 1994. Mirror-polished stainless steel. Photo: Tom Vack.

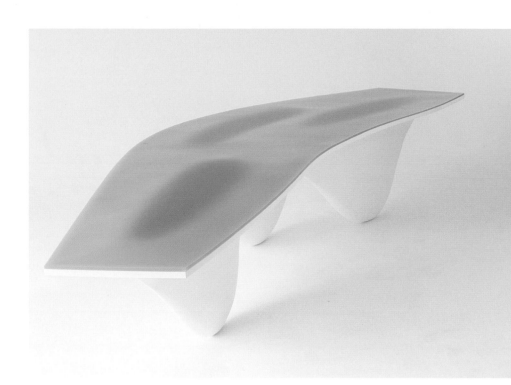

Aqua table, designed by Zaha
Hadid, edition of 12 manufactured
by Established & Sons, UK, 2005.
Laminated and matt polyurethane
resin, silicone. Photo: David Sykes.

IT seating, designed by Jakob
& MacFarlane, manufactured by
Sawaya & Moroni, Italy, 2004.
Fibreglass, resin. Photo: Enrico
Suà Ummarino/Santi Caleca.

service in 1995). The sweeping planes and shard-like character of much of her architecture has led Hadid to be described as a deconstructionist. Latterly compound curves entered her vocabulary as computers have infiltrated her design process. Reduced to the scale of furniture, her forms were highly refined miniature landscapes that looked honed by wind and weather. She called them 'Z-scapes', but in this context they are undoubtedly Blobjects. Hadid morphed a table, divans, a bench and shelves from a unified block 5 metres (16ft 6in) long, conceived as an environment somewhere between furniture and the room that contains it.[24] At 4 metres (13ft) long, her Aqua table was equally monumental. Its three legs, made of laminated polyurethane resin, were like pendulous blisters suspended below the plane of the translucent blue-green silicone table top, through which their internal shadowy voids were half detected like the depths of the ocean. The folding of surfaces into volumes related the table to Hadid's architecture, as exemplified by the Phaeno Science Centre in Wolfsburg she was completing at the time. The Aqua table was the centrepiece of the first collection by Established & Sons, a new British manufacturer launched in 2005 that also made Chester, a sofa that looked like a partially melted traditional chesterfield. Chester was designed by Amanda Levete of Future Systems, an architectural practice whose work, such as Selfridges in Birmingham, had popularized Blobjects at the scale of buildings.

Two designs by Jakob & MacFarlane for Sawaya & Moroni were luxurious, decadent neo-Pop Blobjects. Dominique Jakob and Brendan MacFarlane are Paris-based architects, best known for the Georges Restaurant that transformed the top floor of the Pompidou Centre into a 'blobscape' in 2000. The IT seat (2004) was like a vast sphere that had been eroded, rather like Hadid's furniture. Because of its size it was an organic pod-like micro-environment to clamber into, not a chair to perch on. Their shelves, called Three-One and Three-Two (2003), were made of slotted grids of bright translucent acrylic in vaguely arboreal, branched forms.

Patricia Urquiola is one of the most prolific furniture designers working today, and many of her designs for upholstery for Moroso and others have ingredients I have defined as 'neo-Pop'. The asymmetrical, pod-like Fjord chair (2002), for example, was all curves. It recalled the form of a mid-century modernist icon – Arne Jacobsen's Egg chair – and even had a hint of a radius corner.[25] The Japanese designers Setsu and Shinobu Ito designed Au for Edra (2003), two freeform polyurethane seats similar to Yin and Yang symbols that could be wrapped

Fjord Chair, designed by Patricia Urquiola, manufactured by Moroso, Italy, 2002. Steel frame with injected cold foam padding and leather upholstery. Photo: courtesy of Moroso.

Body Props, designed by Olivier Peyricot, 2001, prototype by VIA, France, 2002, manufactured by Edra, Italy, 2003. Polyurethane foam. Photo: IDSland.

Au seats, designed by Setsu and Shinobu Ito, manufactured by Edra, Italy, 2003. Polyurethane foam with wool and leather upholstery. Photo: courtesy of Edra.

around one another or stand alone. They were organic, like two halves of a cell that had just divided, and their stubby forms seemed to have life and imply motion. Shona Kitchen and Ab Rogers, British architects designing as KRD, designed Monster also for Edra (2000), inspired by the strange, jelly-like creatures of science fiction. Monster was an evolution of a cushion into a lounging environment: a pod for the floor. Olivier Peyricot's Body Props (2003) were also floor-bound. He conceived them as moulded extensions to the body, supporting the spine as sports shoes mould around the feet to aid performance. 'I thought of living in a house as a physical exercise', he said. 'In sport the body offers an increasingly unbelievable performance. "Body props" are an invitation to conquer space as in a sport competition.'[26] The five variant Body Props had the look and feel of bones. Another Peyricot design called 'Wear Your Seat' was like a padded turtle shell that could be worn on the back, ready to cushion and support the body wherever and whenever the user sat down. Furniture has always been a micro-architecture that intercedes between the human body and the environment. With these devices, furniture dissolved until it became a prosthetic that allowed the body to merge with the landscape. Even as I write Blobjects continue to mutate; their bulbous curves harden off to become more faceted and fractured, like crystals or fractals. Konstantin Grcic's chairs for Magis, Moroso and Plank were amongst the first in this trend, as were those by Patricia Urquiola. The Bouroullec brothers explored crystalline shapes for chairs, manufactured by Ligne Roset in France. This furniture still marries the organic and the technological, though the organic metaphor has become mineral rather than vegetal.

Furniture that looks like molten goo, bubbles, happy cartoon characters and amoebic life forms is everywhere today. The retro urge has faded and, at last, fewer designers are seeking solace in the futuristic fantasies of the past. The new Pop paradigms are the blob and the crystal, inspired by natural growth and computer generation in equal measure. How computer-aided design and new materials helped to shape furniture is the subject of the next chapter.

Facett armchair, designed by Ronan and Erwan Bouroullec, manufactured by Ligne Roset, France, 2005. Wood and foam structure with cast ABS arms, upholstery. Photo: Paul Tahon and Ronan Bouroullec.

Marc Newson

Hysterie boutique, Frankfurt, 1992.
Photo: Tom Vack.

Marc Newson became the pin-up boy of furniture in his twenties, epitomizing glamorous, media-driven design. His fashionable fame was cemented by glittering commissions: the design of the livery of a private jet, for example, or the interiors of Simon le Bon's Tokyo recording studio. Concept cars, his own wristwatch brand and 'destination' boutiques, bars and restaurants have all followed. Newson trained as a jeweller, but it was as a furniture designer that he became best known, even though he claims 'being confined to furniture is a bore' and he only gives it 5 per cent of his time now. [1]

The Lockheed Lounge (1986), a chaise longue conceived like a giant piece of jewellery, with 2,000 rivets pinning aluminium plates all over its fibreglass shell, was amongst his first furniture. Two great media manipulators of their age championed its photogenic looks: Philippe Starck put it in the Paramount Hotel and Madonna starred with it in her video for 'Rain'. Its looks and name recalled old aircraft and science fiction, popular culture influences Newson explored with other furniture and interiors designed during a peripatetic period in Tokyo, Paris and

London through the late 1980s and 1990s. In the early 1990s Newson's furniture took on a characteristic hourglass shape he called the 'Orgone', after the meditation pod proposed by the sexologist William Reich. Often Newson would combine the sensuous curves of the Orgone with sensual holes and hollows, seen in the Event Horizon tables, the Orgone chaise longue and the Felt chairs. He claimed: 'Leaving spaces means you can see how things work, it means you are not hiding anything. It gives a dynamic impression of your work. It's almost like a fourth dimension.'[2] Newson has always regarded himself as a craftsman, and his working method is an exploration of materials through hands-on experimentation. This is borne out by his late adoption of computer-aided design, which even then is a tool he leaves to his collaborator, the American architect Benjamin de Haan. But Newson's aesthetic is about the surface, not the structure, and because of this, and the science-fiction set-design quality he consciously evokes, he has found it difficult to overcome accusations that he is a stylist, and to be accepted as a serious designer. It appears to surprise Newson that he is not regarded as a minimalist, like Jasper Morrison, a designer who greatly admires the discipline of Newson's furniture design.[3] A closer inspection of Newson's furniture shows clear and simple ideas pared back to pure forms, not the retro-modern Pop design one expects to find at first glance. Science fiction and science fact blur in some Newson designs. For the Fondation Cartier in Paris, Newson designed the Bucky dome, a structure of interconnected stools to create the form of a Buckminster Fullerine, a form of 60 carbon atoms arranged in a ball, discovered in 1985 and named after the American designer of futuristic geodesic domes.

With the exception of a few plastic items for the French mail order catalogue *Les Trois Suisses* (the Gelo table, 1994) and for Magis, Newson's output has tended to be elite and expensive, though like many designers he wishes this were not so. 'What I want is for my mother to be able to go into a shop in Australia and buy an object that I designed.'[4]

Gluon Chair, manufactured by Moroso, Italy, 1993, injection-moulded polyurethane, sides in rigid coated polyurethane, soft foam upholstery, tubular steel legs. Photo: Sameli Rantanen.

Bucky stool installation, Fondation Cartier pour l'art contemporain, Paris, 1995. Forty chair elements comprising two-thirds of a sphere, injection-moulded polyurethane foam over steel structure, electro-staticly flocked. Photo: Christophe Kicherer.

Tom Dixon

Green Marble table, 2004, Copper
Shade light, 2005, Soft System sofa,
2005, manufactured by Tom Dixon,
UK. Photo: Yuval Hen.

Tom Dixon has travelled from the margins
of design right to the centre of the mainstream. In the 1980s he made one-off furniture
from things he found in skips to show in
galleries, but 20 years later he holds one
of the most visible design posts in Britain,
as Creative Director of high-street furnishing
retailer Habitat.

Dixon proudly announces that his only
qualification is a one-day course in plastic
bumper repair. He dropped out of Chelsea
School of Art after a motorbike accident, and
his design education took place less formally,
making objects for the burgeoning warehouse
party scene and playing bass guitar in a band.
Basically self-taught, and with a background
in music and fashion, he was set apart from his
contemporaries, who were generally educated
at art or architecture schools. His early works
were not designed on paper but grew almost
organically from the process of welding, and
he has always enjoyed the craftsmanship of
making objects himself. Such designs as the
'S' chair of 1987 were equally suited to serial
production (in this case, by Cappellini in

Italy), and increasingly Dixon moved from making objects to designing for industrial production.

Two themes recur throughout Dixon's work and on the surface they can seem contradictory. Recycling, reuse and sustainability have always been important to Dixon, and he has been a significant voice in the argument for 'green' design. His early works were assemblages of found components that spoke loudly and with vigour of the possibilities of recycling. Latterly sustainability has become integral to his design process, and expresses itself with more sophistication – for example, the Eco Ware bio-degradable plastic tableware made of 85 per cent bamboo. The second theme seems to run counter to this model of responsible design, and is associated with the glitz and glamour of Pop designers such as Verner Panton (with whom Dixon shares a fascination for geometric forms and reflective surfaces), and with what can best be described as a 'night club aesthetic'. The Jacklights (see page 66) and other rotation-moulded designs in bright candy colours, and more recent mirrored and reflective designs such as the Mirror Ball lights and the Wire Series tables and chairs, belong here.

Connecting both strands of Dixon's work is a love of manufacturing processes. As detailed elsewhere in this book, Dixon's experiments with plastic have been significant, most notably the Fresh Fat project that re-imagined molten plastic as a hand-craft medium. Many of his industrial products

actually derive from deceptively simple means – for example, the chairs he designed in 2005 that employed rubber bands for upholstery. This reductive solution to a design problem enabled Dixon to marry the responsibility of the ecologically minded designer with the desirability of the Pop object.

Tom Dixon's conversion from maverick to mainstream was completed by his appointment as Head of Design at Habitat in 1998 (and Creative Director since 2001) and an OBE for services to design in 2000. As a major international retailer Habitat gave Dixon access to markets and techniques that had eluded him, and also freed him from the ghetto of 'elite design' that is often forced upon the independent designer-maker. At Habitat Dixon was able to champion the next generation of designers, including Azumi and Tord Boontje. Dixon formed his own company (with David Begg) in 2001 to design and manufacture under his own name, and in 2004 this company merged with the Finnish manufacturer Artek to form Art & Technology.

Fresh Fat furniture, manufactured by Tom Dixon, UK, 2001. Eastman Provista co-polyester. Photo: Gideon Hart.

Wire chair, manufactured by Tom Dixon, UK, 2004. Stainless steel. Photo: Gideon Hart.

Fat chair, manufactured by Cappellini, Italy, 1992. Steel rod with rush upholstery. V&A: W.5-1993, given by Cappellini.

Louis Ghost armchair, designed
by Philippe Starck, manufactured
by Kartell, Italy, 2002. Injection-
moulded polycarbonate. Photo:
courtesy of Kartell.

Air chair, design by Jasper
Morrison, coming out of the mould,
manufactured by Magis, Italy 1999.
Photo: Ramak Fazel/Domus.

Chapter Four

Material Experiments

'Working today with traditional materials is an anachronistic contradiction. It is as if a man from the twenty-first century were to walk around wearing medieval armour.'[1]

Gaetano Pesce

Gaetano Pesce's experiments with materials over four decades inform and inspire generations of younger designers. He uses modern materials from industry, such as foams, resins and plastics, but in a 'craft' way, to create one-off, individualized furniture. At the opposite extreme, Philippe Starck pushes the boundaries of the same materials and industrial processes to populate the world with high-quality, high-design, low-cost multiples. Pesce and Starck – one a craftsman, the other an industrial designer – represent the opposing poles around which much contemporary furniture design pivots. This chapter is about recent furniture that derives from experiments with materials or technical advances, ranging from the diverse ways plastic and wood can be handled, to high-tech materials such as carbon fibre and the possibilities presented by digital technologies. It is important to note that individual designers and large-scale manufacturers experiment in these ways for very different reasons. For the designers, experiments are part of their personal line of enquiry, but most industrialists will only innovate if they are assured of a more cost- or time-efficient production process as an outcome.

Plastic furniture, particularly chairs, has become very low cost and readily available, but has remained associated with cheapness and poor quality, fit only for the garden.[2] The challenge for designers and manufacturers has been to rehabilitate plastic as a material in the minds of consumers, an ongoing project begun with chairs by Verner Panton, Vico Magistretti

MT3 chair, designed by Ron Arad, manufactured by Driade, Italy, 2005. Rotation-moulded polyethylene. Photo: courtesy of Driade / Ron Arad Associates.

Canyon chair, designed by One Foot Taller, manufactured by Harrold Contemporary Furniture, UK, 1999. Rotation-moulded polyethylene. Photo: courtesy of Harrold Contemporary Furniture.

and Joe Colombo in the 1960s. Philippe Starck has long seen the potential of plastic chairs, and even wrote a poem about them.

> I dream weird dreams
> I dream of chairs
> Rather than weep
> I have made them my trade
> While on a Paris-Tokyo flight
> – too long – I dreamt of a small
> solid chair,
> so serviceable and considerate,
> she wanted to be plastic
> and not kill trees[3]

In the 15 years or so since he wrote this poem Starck designed countless plastic chairs, using his considerable clout as the world's most famous designer to persuade manufacturers to invest in the very expensive moulds and machinery required to make them. Single mouldings negate assembly costs and the need for hand-finishing, and have become the holy grail of furniture production. Starck achieved this most spectacularly with a series of chairs that included Toy (1999), made of polypropylene by Driade Atlantide, and La Marie (1998) and Louis Ghost (2002), moulded from polycarbonate by Kartell, both in Italy. La Marie also introduced transparency, as if the chair were cast in glass. It spawned variations by Starck himself for Kartell and numerous look-alikes for rival manufacturers.[4] The icy perfection of polycarbonate, and Starck's rendering of quasi-eighteenth-century forms, elevated the status of the humble plastic chair from the pub beer garden to the luxurious height of the Salon. They were popular, too: by 2005, 100,000 Louis Ghost chairs had been made.[5]

Other designers did not rely on historicism to endow their plastic chairs with kudos. Jasper Morrison developed the Air chair (1997–9) with Magis, another Italian plastics specialist, using technology developed in the automotive industry. The form of the chair, the thicknesses of the plastic and even the position and direction of the injection points were all calculated in advance by computer simulations. In a single moulding, polypropylene strengthened with glass fibre was injected into the mould, as were precision-calculated chambers of air that gave the chair its name and also its lightness. The air chambers left ribs between them that created the invisible skeleton of the chair. The tooling for such a chair required immense investment, but a successful design reaps rewards for its manufacturer: each Air chair took just four minutes

Nobody's shelves, designed by
Gaetano Pesce, manufactured
by Zerodisegno, Italy, 2002,
polyurethane resin, V&A: W.63-
2002, given by Quattrocchio S.r.L.;
Crosby child's chair, designed
by Gaetano Pesce, manufactured
by Fish Design, New York, 1998,
moulded resin, V&A: W.51-2005,
given by Bettina and Joe Gleason.

to fabricate and by 2006 in excess of 350,000 had been manufactured. Magis extended the Air family with stools, tables and trolleys, a folding chair and in 2005, an armchair.[6]

Not all plastic technology requires such high levels of tooling and investment. Rotation moulding is simpler and cheaper, and uses centrifugal force to spread polyethylene around the inside of a spinning mould. The results tend to be cruder than injection moulding, often bearing mould marks and with variable thicknesses of plastic, but they are durable and, most importantly, inexpensive. Conventionally rotation moulding is the technique used to make traffic bollards and other street furniture, and Tom Dixon was surprised how low-tech it was when he explored the technology in about 1996. He had already put wire and paper lamps into production but was eager to develop something that was easier to make. The Jacklight (see p.66) grew from the shape of these lamps. Rotation moulding is simple enough to allow for small production runs: the first Jacklights were fabricated by a maker of agricultural machinery in Somerset, a far cry from the hubbub of the Milan Furniture Fair. Yet for Dixon the Jacklight signalled a new direction, affording him access to batch production he had not gained before.

Once the Jacklight introduced rotation moulding to furniture design, other designers rapidly adopted the technique, including Richard Hutten in Rotterdam and Glasgow-based designers One Foot Taller, who enjoyed considerable media attention with their Canyon, Ravine and Chasm chairs (1998–9). Undercuts are impossible with rotation moulding, but they overcame this by splitting the plastic from top to bottom, and re-attaching the two parts the opposite way round, leaving the empty centre visible from the sides. It may be cheap, but rotation moulding is slower than other techniques, so Ron Arad designed a form that could be cut in half vertically to make two chairs in one go (Nino Rota and None Rota, designed with Yukiko Tango for Cappellini, 2002). They were not entirely resolved, but a more satisfying design was his MT chair for Italian furniture manufacturer Driade in 2005. The name was a pun on the Empty Chair, Arad's first product for Driade, and on the empty centre that lay at the heart of the rotation-moulded chair. In this instance the sides were sliced from the plastic moulding to reveal the inside surface, rendered in a different colour polyethylene. Rotation moulding became a popular process for small-scale

Chair, designed and made by Bär
& Knell, Germany, 1996. Recycled
post-consumer plastic packaging,
V&A: W.12-1996.

designer-makers in the late 1990s and 2000s, eager to access industrial processes, as well as an economic technology for the mass-producers. The only limit has been the maximum size of the moulds, which is about 3.5 metres (11ft 6in) in diameter.

Gaetano Pesce is not concerned with designing furniture that could be moulded in endlessly repeatable identical units. Plastics are generally moulded in sealed moulds, but for the Open Sky collections that Pesce developed in his own Fish Design studio in New York, and commercially with the Italian manufacturer Zerodisegno (2002), the mould was open to the sky, enabling him to intervene as the plastic was being formed, stirring in different colours, adding other materials or fragments, or marking the object with hand-writing. The results looked fluid and random, as if the plastic were still molten, but they were controlled effects. They were deliber-ately imperfect: Pesce called a related collect-ion of furniture 'Nobody's Perfect'. Elsewhere Pesce experimented with dripped urethanes and resins to make freeform and often monu-mental one-off objects. These were made in lurid, even putrid colours, but Pesce's singular aesthetic makes his work instantly recognizable and highly collectable.

Aside from using rags impregnated with resins to make his Seaweed furniture (1991), Pesce has not engaged with issues of recycling. Yet he has influenced the debate about reuse and sustainability of materials in furniture design, most notably in the work of Bär and Knell from Germany and Jane Atfield in London, during the mid-1990s. Both designers reused plastics. Gerhard and Beata Bär and Hartmut Knell made chairs by melting layers of waste plastic packaging over a form to produce a rigid, draped shape. The logos and colours of the original packaging were clearly visible and intentionally so, since the design-ers' chief intent was for the work to stand as an indictment of our over-consumption and wastefulness. Formally, the furniture looked molten, and each chair in the series was individual, owing much to Pesce's manner of working. Jane Atfield found an American company, Yemm and Hart in Marquand, Missouri, who made board from chipped recycled post-consumer plastic. She imported the technique to Britain, manufacturing the board under the name 'Made of Waste'. The board was self-coloured by the particular mix of plastics it contained, but more evenly than either Pesce's or Bär and Knell's plastics. Her furniture had simple plank structures in the architectonic manner of Gerrit Rietveld,

RCP2 chair, designed by Jane Atfield, manufactured by Made of Waste, UK, 1994, recycled plastic board. V&A: W.4-1996.

allowing the brightly coloured recycled plastic to dominate the design, which thus became a manifesto about the need to recycle. It stood at the crossroads of industrial manufacturing and small-scale production, and was an original note in the handling of plastic.[7] Other interesting forays into sustainable materials include hybrid 'organic plastics'. One example is Alberto Lievore's Rothko chair (1989–94) made in Spain of 'maderón', a plastic wood material derived from discarded almond shells (a by-product of processing the nuts for the food industry). Similarly, Tom Dixon's Ecoware (2003) is bio-degradable tableware with a five year life, made of polyamide-bound bamboo fibre plastic.

Pesce's influence was felt in the Netherlands too. In 1999 Bertjan Pot designed the Shrunken stool, and with fellow Dutchman Daniel White, he produced stools and benches under the name 'the Monkey Boys'. The furniture looked mutated and deformed, like some of Pesce's work. The seats were made of polystyrene blocks inserted into resin-soaked fabric tubes. When they were placed in a vacuum chamber, the resin was drawn from the fabric into the polystyrene, bonding the cover to the substrate and hardening it. The shape of the object also mutated as the polystyrene lost 10 per cent of its volume, meaning each piece of furniture was unique. Lightweight and durable artefacts with great individuality were created from ubiquitous modern materials and a relatively low-fi technology.[8]

Tom Dixon's success with rotation moulding encouraged him to embark on more radical experiments with plastic in 2001. Plastic extrusion machines generally inject molten plastic directly into a mould. Dixon's innovation was to omit the mould and form objects directly from the filament of plastic as it emerged from the nozzle of the machine, rather like icing a cake. He settled on Provista Copolymer, a resin made by Eastman with a very clear, glass-like quality, high strength and a glossy surface. There was no limit to the size of the object that could be formed, because there were no moulds. The only constraint was the speed at which the plastic thread could be positioned, as it quickly hardened and would also bond on contact. In this respect the analogy of blowing glass by hand is useful, as hot glass performs in much the same way as molten plastic. The chairs, tables, large bowls and other objects that Dixon called the 'Fresh Fat' collection were like three-dimensional scribbles, dynamically capturing the fluidity of the material at the

Rothko chair, designed by Alberto Lievore, 1989–94, manufactured by Indartu, Spain, 1996. Maderón composite material. V&A: W.13-1996, given by the Maderón Promotion Agency.

Fresh Fat chair being constructed
from extruded Provista Copolymer
resin, 2002. Photo: courtesy
of Tom Dixon.

Shrunken bench, designed by
Bertjan Pot, manufactured by the
Monkey Boys, the Netherlands,
2002. Polystyrene, resin impregnated
textile, V&A: W.60-2002.

moment it was extruded. Like Pesce, Dixon found a way to make customized, unique objects with a material and technique intended for the mass-production of uniform products.

It is very easy to accept automatically the validity of new materials because of their association with modernity, but Philippe Starck sounds a note of caution. 'The idea of modernity is... not only a question of materials. If you made a table out of carbon fibre, it might seem the *non plus ultra* of modernity, but it would in fact be a pointless and uninteresting piece of baroque furniture.'[9] Yet carbon fibre has found applications in contemporary furniture, despite its extremely high cost in comparison to other materials. Carbon fibre, usually woven into a cloth or embedded in epoxy to stiffen it, is amongst the lightest and strongest materials and this, combined with its glossy black appearance, endears it to furniture designers. It was developed for the

aeronautic, space and automotive industries, where strength-weight ratios are important factors. More latterly it has found applications in consumer goods and sports equipment for similar reasons, including fishing rods, laptop computers and bicycles. Starck's objection was that carbon fibre is too highly specified for the purpose at hand: a table does not need to perform like a Formula One car. His comment was a sideswipe at Ron Arad and Marc Newson, both of whom designed furniture made from the material. Arad has often translated designs from one material to another and enjoyed the irony that his heavy steel pieces were made ultra-light using carbon fibre.[10]

For a time designers competed to make the lightest possible chair from carbon fibre. One of the first was the Lightlight chair by the Italian designer Alberto Meda for the Italian furniture manufacturer Alias (1987),

Black Hole table, designed by
Marc Newson, manufactured
by Idée, Japan, 1988. Carbon fibre
on a structure of rigid polyurethane
and Nomex honeycomb. Photo:
courtesy of Marc Newson.

Spun Carbon chaise longue,
designed by Mathias Bengtsson,
self production, UK, 2003.
Carbon fibre. Photo: courtesy
of Phillips, de Pury & Company.

made of moulded carbon fibre fabric sandwiched around Nomex, a honeycomb core. Meda, an engineer, brought great technical skill to the design of the chair, which he followed up with the Softlight chair in 1989. Another contender, Pol Quadens' CO6 chair of 1995, weighed in at just 980g (34½oz). Quadens, a former coach restorer, made the chair himself, claiming it was the lightest chair in the world, but failed to find an industrial manufacturer to take it on.[11] The Wing chair (2000) was designed in-house by the research team at Poltrona Frau in Italy, and took its name from the aircraft wing profile of the legs. A veritable heavyweight at 2.4kg (just over 5lb), the Wing chair was made of moulded carbon fibre fabric with injected polyurethane foam in the seat and back for comfort.

Mathias Bengtsson's prototype chaise longue (2003) was made using technology developed by NASA. A robotic arm spun a continuous thread of carbon fibre around a mould to create a cylindrical form not dissimilar in shape to Marc Newson's Orgone furniture.[12] It looked very high-tech, befitting the nature of the material. In the hands of two Dutch designers, however, carbon fibre was used with wit and irony. One of the most iconic recent chairs was Marcel Wanders' Knotted chair (1996), made of rope wound around a carbon core, hardened with epoxy. It had the appearance of hand-knotted macramé but also incredible strength and durability. The chair grew out of a project called Dry Tech, a collaboration that aimed to combine the rough-and-ready low-tech aesthetics of Droog Design with the high-tech materials of the Aviation and Space Laboratory of Delft University of Technology. Bertjan Pot, an acolyte of Wanders, made a copy of the Eameses' Plastic chair of 1950 from strands of carbon fibre and appropriately called it 'Carbon Copy' (2003).[13] The Plastic chair had been the first to celebrate unadorned polyester reinforced with glass fibre. In fact

Knotted chair, designed by
Marcel Wanders, 1996, manufactured
by Cappellini, Italy, 2005. Aramid
fibres around a carbon core, impregnated with epoxy. V&A: W.49-2005,
given by Cappellini and Marcel
Wanders.

Pot's chair was much closer in spirit to the Eameses' Wire Mesh chairs of 1951, which translated the Plastic chair's shell into an open metal structure. In 2004 Pot reworked his design with Marcel Wanders to create the Carbon chair, manufactured by Moooi. The strands of carbon fibre looked randomly positioned, but actually reflected the tension patterns of the chair.

Charles and Ray Eames chose plastics and wire because they connoted modernity and enabled affordable mass production. Although in its own way carbon fibre is the material of our age, to date it remains too expensive for mass-production applications. In the immediate post-war years the Eameses recalled: 'If you looked around you found these fantastic things being made of wire - trays, baskets, rat traps, using a wire fabricating technique perfected over a period of many years. We looked into it and found that it was a good production technique and also a good use of material.'[14] Half a century later Shin and Tomoko Azumi worked with a manufacturer of shopping baskets and supermarket trolleys to make wire furniture for exactly the same reasons.

Born in 1979, the Dutch designer Peter Traag is one of the youngest furniture designers to find their work in this book. Having graduated from the Arnhem Academy of Art and Design, the Alma Mater of Marcel Wanders and Dick van Hoff, Traag joined Ron Arad's Design Products course at the Royal College of Art, studying on platforms run by Tord Boontje and Daniel Charny and graduating in 2003. Traag said his Sponge chair, developed at the RCA, was more of 'an accident than a controlled design'. It was formed by pouring liquid polyurethane foam directly into the upholstery, which was 150 per cent bigger than the flexible PVC mould that contained it.[15] The foam cured in just ten minutes, and removed from the mould, the

Carbon chair, designed by Bertjan Pot and Marcel Wanders, manufactured by Moooi, the Netherlands, 2004. Carbon fibre and epoxy. Photo: Maarten van Houten.

chair's characteristic rhinoceros wrinkles were permanently set. Gaetano Pesce had experimented with pouring polyurethane foam directly into upholstery with his Sit Down chairs (Cassina, 1975–6) but the results were more freeform since he did not use a mould. Traag regarded his work as halfway between the expressive, individual experiments of Pesce and the low-cost, standardized products designed by Starck. The architect Will Alsop was invited to curate an exhibition at the Valencia Furniture Fair in 2003 and asked Ron Arad to propose student work. Arad put forward Traag's chair, Massimo Morozzi saw it in Valencia and in 2004 his company Edra began to manufacture it.

Elsewhere Traag combined his material experiments with appropriated components; a hybrid of Italian and Dutch design sensibilities, perhaps. The Mummy chair (Edra, 2005), for example, wrapped an archetypal bentwood chair with 60 metres (200ft) of elasticated webbing over foam. The wrapping, and the type of chair that was wrapped, were very reminiscent of Jurgen Bey's Kokon furniture (1997, see p.36). The Kokon Furniture was another outcome of the Dry Tech project that had given rise to Wanders' Knotted chair the previous year. Here, a technique from the aeronautic industry was adopted whereby a PVC coating was spun over the object forming a skin that could span open areas. It shrank and tightened, but remained flexible. Traag wanted to upholster a common chair to make it more comfortable, but Bey's chair

Wire Frame chair and stool, designed by Shin and Tomoko Azumi, self-production, UK, 1998. Prefabricated mesh and steel rod, powder-coated. Photo: Yasuyuki Sakurai.

Sponge chair, designed by Peter Traag, manufactured by Edra, Italy, 2004. Polyurethane foam formed within the polyester upholstery. Photo: courtesy of Edra.

Vermelha chair, designed by
Humberto and Fernando Campana,
manufactured by Edra, Italy, 1993–8.
Powder-coated steel frame with
woven acrylic and cotton rope
upholstery. Photo: courtesy of Edra.

Gel chair, designed by Werner
Aisslinger, manufactured
by Cappellini, Italy, 2002,
gel upholstery, metal frame.
Photo: courtesy of Werner
Aisslinger.

was about the concept of giving new life to a discarded object.

As demonstrated by the Sponge chair, Edra is prepared to experiment and innovate with the materials and techniques it uses. Ross Lovegrove's Air One chair (2001) was not made of polystyrene, as it appeared, but moulded polypropylene foam. It is equally lightweight but far stronger and is most often used in car fascias and door panels to absorb shocks. Edra also developed semi-transparent upholstery fabrics, made of polyester fibres and polyurethane resin, or latex film, and teamed them with natural fillers such as linen fibres, creating strange hybrid upholstery that mixed synthetics and organics. Massimo Morozzi used it for the Hi Square sofa in 1995.

Like Peter Traag, the Brazilian brothers Fernando and Humberto Campana owe much of their success to Edra and many of their works have been unconventionally upholstered. They specialize in low-tech solutions, or unlikely combinations of materials. The design that launched their international careers was the Vermelha chair (1993–8), for which 500 metres (1,640ft) of rope were handwoven onto a steel frame with sufficient surplus to leave loose loops in what appeared to be a random tangle. The back of the Campanas' Bamboo chair (2000), for Hidden, was made of a cluster of freestanding upright bamboo stems that flexed independently when they were lent on. The bamboo was cropped at shoulder height, and the chairs were a more orderly version of the Eyelash chair by Polish designer Pawel Grunert (about 2000), which had a back rest of natural wicker stems standing over 2 metres (6ft 6in) tall, like untrimmed cousins of Andrea Branzi's Domestic Animals.[16] Both the Campanas and Grunert exploited the rawness of their raw materials. By 2005 the Brazilians' Bamboo chair, however, had a new incarnation at Edra as the Jenette chair with PVC rods replacing the bamboo back of the original, losing much impact in translation.

The German designer Werner Aisslinger prefers new materials. He worked for both Ron Arad and Jasper Morrison in London, returned to Berlin in 1993 and was the first designer, in 1999, to experiment with gel as an upholstery material. Gel pads spread body weight and reduce pressure points, giving more comfort than sprung or foam padding, and have the additional appeal to the designer of transparency. Aisslinger's self-produced Soft-Cell furniture used Levagel®, a polyurethane derivative made by Bayer for medical applications and also employed to cushion bicycle seats and computer accessories. The furniture had an open cell structure that let light through. The following year he refined the idea with the Italian manufacturer Zanotta, using an Italian gel known as Technogel, for the Soft chaise longue. Two years later, Aisslinger's Gel lounge chair was launched by Cappellini who reported selling 30 to Brad Pitt for his Santa Barbara beach house. French designer Christian Ghion also used gel for his Blue Lagoon chaise, though with less refinement than Aisslinger.[17]

Remaining with upholstery, the innovation found in Michael Young's Smartie pouf for Cappellini (1998) was that it did not have a cover at all. Moulded around a polystyrene core were several centimetres of flexible self-coating and self-coloured polyurethane. Unlike a traditional fabric cover, the surface remained wrinkle-free, even over the compound curves of the little domed stools.[18] Edra had used self-coating polyurethane for Maarten van Severen's slab-like sofa the previous year. Earlier still, Marc Newson's Bucky seats, made to connect together to form a geodesic dome as an installation in the Fondation Cartier, Paris, had a flocked surface electrostatically applied to the polyurethane foam pad (1995, see page 87).[19] Other innovative upholstery experiments included Ineke Hans's Magic chair in 2002, in which woven glass fibre was successfully bonded to a foam substrate: it was both soft and very strong. Recalling the pleated fabrics developed by his mentor Issey Miyake, Tokujin Yoshioka's Boing series for Driade (2005) was upholstered in finely pleated leather.

Japanese designer Tokujin Yoshioka took a poetic approach to making a paper chair. The Honey-Pop chair (2001) was like a concertina-folded paper lantern or Christmas decoration, made of a special high-strength paper. It folded open from flat, and the first person to sit in it crushed the paper to form the seat. Almost miraculously the concertina structure was strong enough to bear the weight of a person. Like much of the most interesting recent furniture, the Honey-Pop chair was not complete until the user had intimately interacted with it. It was not intended to be a commercial design but was more like an art piece. Yoshioka was not alone in experimenting with paper to make furniture. Frank Gehry famously used cardboard for chairs in the early 1970s and these were reissued by Vitra in 2005. In France, Olivier Leblois designed a die-cut cardboard chair

Honey-Pop chair, designed by Tokujin Yoshioka, 125 of an edition of 300, self-production, Japan, 2001. Glassine paper. V&A: W.5-2005, given by Tokujin Yoshioka.

LaLeggera chair, 1996, Ilvolo table, 2000, designed by Ricardo Blumer, manufactured by Alias, Italy. Solid timber, plywood, polyurethane foam. Photo: courtesy of twentytwentyone.

in 1993; it was made of recycled material, and was totally recyclable at the end of its useful life. Much like packaging, it relied on folds for its structural strength. Leblois used no glue, and the chair was held together using chopsticks. And the British company Lloyd Loom of Spalding revived the technique of woven twisted paper, most popular between the World Wars, with new designs by Nigel Coates, Jane Dillon and others.[20]

Plywood and bentwood have been staple furniture materials for 150 years, yet in the last decade and a half advances in these technologies have still taken place. These largely result from the development of refined fixatives and computer-controlled cutting techniques that together have enabled manufacturers to create more complex plywood shells more accurately, affordably and quickly than before. A good example is the Millefoglie ('thousand leaves') chair by Biagio Cisotti and Sandra Laube, made by the Italian company Plank (1998). The name is taken from a pastry with many fine layers, and refers to the stripes of the chair's veneer. The seat and back of the chair were two identical shells that only took six minutes each to mould, simplifying production.[21] Italian designer Ricardo Blumer's

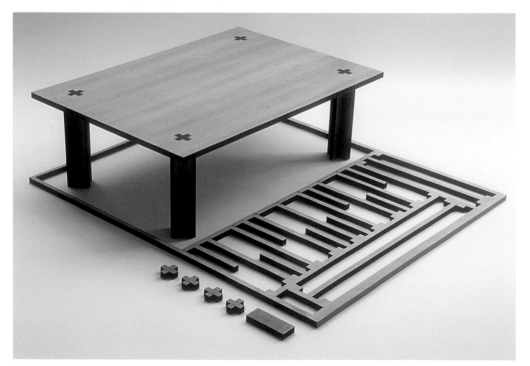

family of chairs, stools, benches and tables (1996–2000) exploited plywood's ratio of weight to strength. Very thin plywood is relatively strong, but it is brittle, especially at exposed edges. Blumer's innovation was to conceive of the furniture as hollow boxes filled with polyurethane foam. The shaped solid timber sides were only 5mm thick while the plywood surfaces were just one millimetre thick. Without the foam the furniture would not be feasible. It cushioned the plywood and gave the furniture structural support while adding very little weight.[22] Vitra's Taino chair by German designer Jacob Gebert refined the moulding of plywood: the aluminium legs were sandwiched inside the veneer layers of the plywood seat, rather than mounted externally. 'Because it is a single unit', he said, 'it is a stronger chair. It's funny, but I found that the connection between wood and metal is better than that between wood and wood.'[23]

Ron Arad's Empty chair for Driade (1993), originally designed for the Belgo Noord restaurant in Chalk Farm, London, was made of plywood curves surrounding a hollow core. Similarly there was nothing at the centre of the Boa chair (G.A. Panizon, M. Martinelli and G. Dorligo, 1996) which was only a 220cm (86in) plywood strip, looped and formed to describe the top and bottom planes of a sideless chair. Made by the Italian company Emmemobili, Boa celebrated plywood. It is extremely difficult to achieve structural rigidity this way and maintain consistent shapes from chair to chair, since plywood is naturally wont to vary from piece to piece and to shift in climatic changes. So its use here was not

for reasons of economy or to reduce the weight of the chair, but to show off the possibilities of the material.

Cork is a by-product of the timber industry, and has been actively promoted as a furniture material as its traditional use for wine-bottle stoppers declines. Spanish designers Roberto Feo and Rosario Hurtado are El Ultimo Grito, a design team based in London. They used cork chips moulded with latex for the body of the Miss Ramirez chair (1997), inspired by Birkenstok shoes that have cork soles and by the Spanish cork industry.[24] In 2004, Jasper Morrison designed cork stools and occasional tables for Vitra, reminiscent of both outsize wine corks and the Eameses' Time Life stools (1960). He followed these up with an outsize cork bowl the following year, also for Vitra. New York-based Kevin Walz designed furniture entirely made of cork under the KorQinc brand, stylistically indebted to Michael Graves' postmodernism.

Across materials, but mostly with timber and plywood, computer numerically controlled (CNC) cutting technology has transformed furniture. Most machine-shop appliances can now be controlled by computer programmes, though mills and lathes are the most popular. The technique offers minute accuracy and the potential to cut very complex patterns. For example, all the elements of the Table with Crossed Legs by British designer Simon Jones could be laser-cut from a single sheet of 18mm MDF (medium-density fibreboard), leaving charred edges that the designer incorporated as a decorative detail. Precision cutting like this obviates the need for fixings or glue: the table's components simply slot together. Ineke Hans used the same technology for her Laser chair (2002) to recreate the fretwork patterns of folk art. She also exploited the burnt cut holes, and blackened her whole chair to match (the chair was part of a collection called 'Black Magic'). The Laser chair found a complement in the Doily table (2004), laser-cut and slotted together from black Perspex, not MDF, but sharing the same highly decorative, pierced aesthetic as Ineke Hans's chair. The Doily table was the first product by young British design team Miscellaneous, graduates of the RCA. The Prince chair by British/Danish designer Louise Campbell continued the trend for black, lace-like furniture. Here, laser-cut sheet steel was faced with neoprene and felt upholstery cut with a high-pressure water jet. Campbell designed it in 2002 for a competition to design a new chair for the Crown Prince of Denmark, and Danish firm Hay

Laser chair, designed by Ineke Hans, self-production, the Netherlands, 2002. Laser-cut MDF. Photo: courtesy of Ineke Hans.

put it into production in 2005.

These designers all used CNC cutting to create complex two-dimensional patterns, part of a decorative trend dominated (and largely instigated) by the work of Tord Boontje. Fellow Dutchman Jeroen Verhoeven, however, pushed the boundaries of CNC cutting to create the Cinderella table in 2005, as part of a project he called 'From Fantasy to Factory'. He designed it while still a student at the Design Academy in Eindhoven (where, incidentally, Tord Boontje had also studied), where he was taught by Hella Jongerius, Jurgen Bey and Dick van Hoff. On graduating in 2005 he set up his own studio in the same Rotterdam building as Richard Hutten. Verhoeven's aim was to rediscover craftsmanship within the industrial process of shaping wood using computerized machinery, and to achieve this he worked with a boatyard. His design morphed together on a computer the outline of a baroque table with that of a bombé commode. Then he divided the form into 57 slices, CNC-cut from both sides to create complex compound curves that were joined to form the complete table, made of 741 plywood layers. It was a virtuoso use of technology in the service of craftsmanship.[25] Computer-Aided Design and its corollary, Computer-Aided Manufacture (CAD-CAM), of which CNC milling is an example, have narrowed the gap between the designer's intention and the realization of the finished product, speeding the design to manufacture process. Many of the technical innovations and material experiments in this chapter have been in the cause of making cheaper, more efficient and more durable furniture. They are but the latest workings of an industrial system that relies on innovation to ensure competitiveness. Rapid prototyping, however, is a new manufacturing process that challenges the very nature of mass-production techniques, and the relationship between unique and serially produced objects.[26]

As its name suggests, rapid prototyping was developed as a tool for industrial designers and manufacturers to accurately and quickly model components in three dimensions, and in its infancy in the 1990s the technology was prohibitively expensive. Like CNC cutting, rapid prototyping is entirely dependent on the interface of a digital design and a tool. In this instance the computer-generated designs are 'sliced' virtually into layers as thin as 0.15mm. Several competing technologies exist to fabricate the objects and one of them, selective laser sintering (SLS), is often described as three-dimensional printing. As thin layers of polyamide powder are laid down on top of each other, computer-controlled laser beams scan the surface corresponding to the layers of the sliced design, and the lasers' heat causes the molecules of the powder to fuse. Over time the three-dimensional object is built up, fused layer by fused layer. Sintered objects have the character of bone and are generally stronger than those made by stereolithography. This process is similar, in that it is operated by computer-controlled lasers following the pattern of the sliced design, but here they scan the surface of a tank of liquid polymer, causing it to harden. As the object is constructed, it is lowered into the tank, so only the top edge is within reach of the laser. A frequently used analogy is that the objects are 'grown' in the rapid prototyping machines, which indeed is how it looks. But the organic metaphor only serves to conceal the utterly digital origins of the technique.

Despite the expense of doing so, both Ron Arad and Marcel Wanders have used

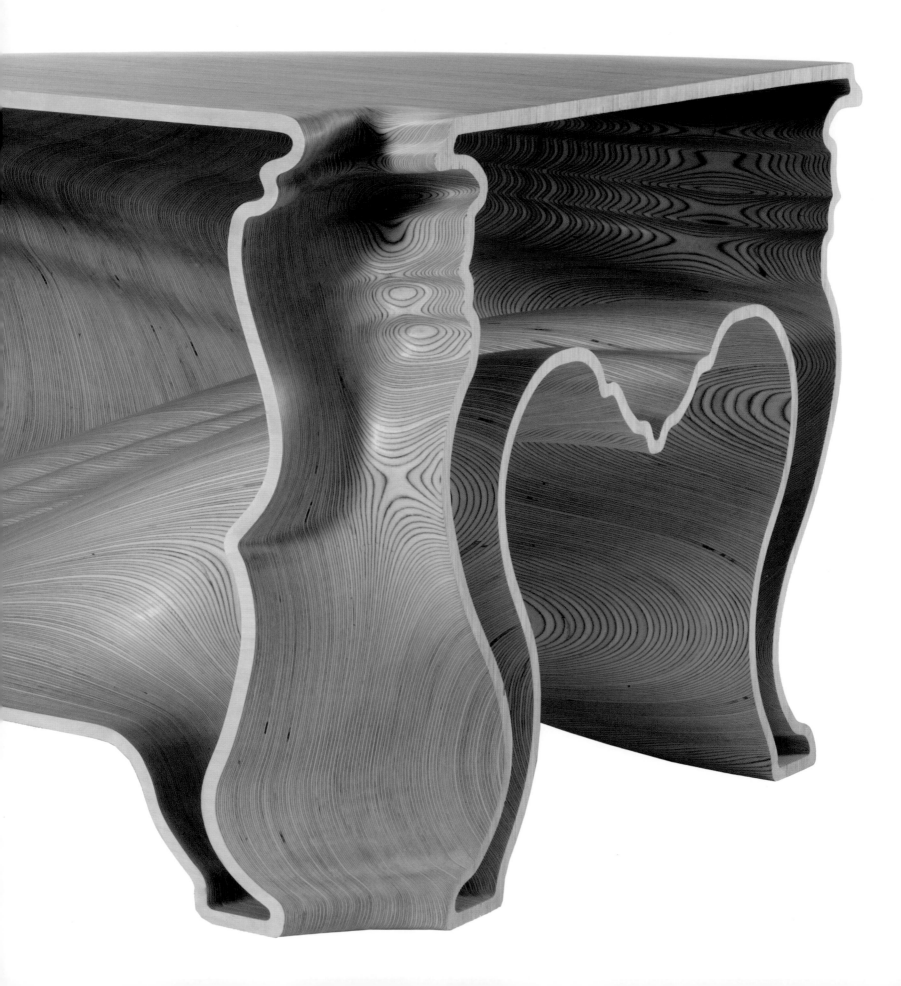

Cinderella table, designed
by Jeroen Verhoeven, edition
of 20 self-production, the
Netherlands, 2005, CNC-cut
plywood. V&A: W.1-2006.

these technologies, not to create prototypes or stages along the path of a product's development, but to fabricate the finished artefacts themselves. The technology means an object can be produced as a single example, or identically in series. Arad combined it with digital animation to create unique objects like frames from a movie, each related to but different from the next. Wanders used microscopy to capture and enlarge the shape of germs invisible to the human eye. For both, the advantage of the technique is that it circumvents the rules controlling plastic moulding, like not having undercuts on the object. Any form can be constructed, even those with extreme undercuts or intertwining forms. The greatest limitation was the size of the tanks in which the objects were 'grown', but in recent years the machines have expanded. Now it is possible to 'grow' entire pieces of furniture, and the first designer to do so, in 2004, was Patrick Jouin. Jouin's 'Solid' project comprised of four objects; a stool, a table base, and two chairs, each totally formed by SLS or stereolithography. The Belgian firm of Materialise dominates the technology, with the largest machines, and fabricated Jouin's designs. He deliberately envisaged objects that could not be moulded or made by any conventional method. Materialise not only fabricates one-off objects and prototypes for industry, it also markets a range of lamps manufactured by rapid prototyping machines.[27]

Conceptually, rapid prototyping appears to subtract a stage of the design process by seeming to conflate prototyping and production. But this is not strictly so, as prototyping shifts towards the beginning of the design process to take place as part of the 3D modelling and testing of a design on screen. More significantly this technology allows for mass customization of designs, wherein each object is made individually and independently, so can be amended digitally at the pre-production stage according to a customer's whim. But equally the technology allows for the production of unlimited amounts of identical units, controlled by the same computer files. The conceptual difference between the unique, crafted object and the serially produced industrial product becomes blurred; the extremes represented by Pesce and Starck have been drawn closer together. As the technology evolves, and particularly as the polyamides and polymers are perfected and become stronger, it will become quite possible to 'grow' unique pieces of furniture that bear no relation to old paradigms,

structural conventions, or constraints of manufacture or of the market. Whether it will ever be economically viable for commercial production runs remains far less certain. Nevertheless, Patrick Jouin's furniture, like the Blobjects of the previous chapter, are the first indicators of the material, technical and industrial changes wrought upon furniture production by digital advances.

Solid chair, designed by
Patrick Jouin, manufactured
by Materialise, Belgium, 2004.
Stereolithography. Photo:
Thomas Duval.

Ron Arad

This Mortal Coil bookcase, manufactured by One Off Ltd, UK, 1993. Mild steel. V&A: W.18-1993.

Big Easy armchair, manufactured by One Off Ltd, UK, 1990. Stainless steel. Photo: Willi Moser.

'I think newness is important. The way ideas go ahead in any area – in fashion, in art, as well as in architecture – is usually by people joining a bandwagon. But I'm more interested in the actual moment of the new, in that time where some things, some objects and ideas get born which weren't there before.' [1]

By focusing on what is new, Ron Arad has created a body of work at the intersection of art and design. In so doing, he has changed the way furniture designers perceive themselves. Not content to be either a marginalized designer-maker, or a jobbing product designer working to a company brief, Arad has drawn from both craft and industry to create a unique space where he can create furniture and objects that initially exist to answer his own exploration of materials, techniques and symbolism. The son of artists, Arad raised the bar for furniture designers by behaving like an artist. Key collaborators have enabled Arad to achieve this, most notably his business partner since 1981, Caroline Thorman, the gallerist Ernest Mourmans, and progressive design-led manufacturers such as Rolf Fehlbaum at Vitra, Patrizia Moroso and Alberto Alessi.

A characteristic of Arad's oeuvre has been to explore a single form in many different media, each with their own qualities, demonstrated by the various versions of the Big Easy

chair, an example of which perches on the roof of his studio like a sign representing his activities. He made the first versions himself in 1989, and they bear his raw welds and hammer marks. Later, skilled specialist metal-workers refined the fabrication, and Arad specified a highly polished surface. These metal chairs were still made to order as part of limited editions and were 'sittable sculp-tures' for collectors as much as they were usable furniture. But Moroso in Italy trans-lated the shape of the steel chair into foam and upholstery for serial production in 1990, introducing it to the international market for contemporary furniture that, though small, was still larger than the collectors' or art market.

With this and other chairs Arad was able to create new limited editions of designs whose editions were exhausted by translating them into different materials, feeding the collectors' market without diluting it. Arad reinterpreted the Big Easy chair by casting it in polyester, which he personally painted into the moulds. They were reminiscent of Abstract Expressionist paintings and he called the series of unique chairs 'New Orleans'. The Big Easy has also been made in carbon fibre and, at the opposite extreme in terms of expense, in rotation-moulded polyethylene too. A single form therefore exists as unique versions, in small numbered batches and as lower cost multiples, and their diversity is almost as if Arad wants to test his ideas to destruction.

Arad's appointment to the Royal College of Art as Professor of Furniture and Industrial Design in 1997 (from 1999, Head of Design Products) also marked his arrival at the centre of design culture from its margins. As an educator he has encouraged his students towards intellectual investigations that have led to many more concepts, but to far less furniture appearing in RCA degree shows. His interest in the conceptual value of objects, and in particular his experiments with the materials and techniques of production, for example rapid prototyping technologies, have made him one of the most influential figures in contemporary design.

Box in Four Movements chair, edition of 20, manufactured by Ron Arad Studio, Italy, 1994. Stainless steel. Photo: Tom Vack.

New Orleans armchair, edition of 18 unique pieces, handmade by Ron Arad for Gallery Mourmans, Belgium, 1999. Polyester reinforced with fibreglass. Photo: Erik Hesmerg.

Gaetano Pesce

Table for the Magasin Dujardin, Brussels, 1992-3. Metal, polyurethane. Photo: courtesy of Phillips, de Pury & Company.

'I offend good taste? Sure, because I am against old taste' [1]

Gaetano Pesce (born 1939) is the most senior designer in this book, not only because he is the oldest, but because his work is central to many of the debates that have shaped furniture design in the last four decades. As far back as 1969 Pesce designed the Up series of expanded foam chairs for C&B Italia, which are widely regarded as modern classics; in 1972 he participated in the agenda-setting exhibition, *Italy, the New Domestic Landscape*; and designs such as the Sit-Down chair (Cassina, 1975) and the Pratt chair (1984) predated and predicted work by younger designers who routinely cite Pesce as a major influence.

Pesce's opposition to the standardization of modernism in part explains the layered, sometimes random appearance of his furniture, interiors and architecture, which cannot be 'read' simply, but which embody complexity. He politicizes the design process by drawing comparisons between the individuated object and the liberated individual. Perhaps this is why many of his objects are anthropomorphic, which at times can also make them somewhat disturbing. In 1994 he designed a Park Avenue apartment to be a literal and metaphysical portrait of his client, and his reconfiguration of offices for the Chiat

Day advertising firm the following year was little short of psychedelic.

A free-thinker, then, Pesce stands for individualism in the face of imposed conformity. He celebrates flaws and irregularities that conventional designers or manufacturers reject. Pesce's playful and decorative inclinations align his work with a younger generation of conceptual designers, and like them he emphasizes the artistic content of his designs over the practical. He designs manifestos. His objects are neither standardized industrial products, nor works of art, but are midway on the continuum that connects both systems. In many ways the times have caught up with him, as the age of mass-production has transformed into the age of mass customization. Or, as Pesce puts it, 'This is the time of non-homogeneous production. And it doesn't only make economic sense but political sense also – democracy is a system that guarantees to maintain difference.'[2]

A common characteristic shared by his design, architecture and art is the sculptural, expressive and freehand use of synthetics and plastics: his favourite medium. Pesce's works could be called 'diversified serial production', and form a commentary on the possibilities of industrial production, because they use the same materials and techniques as mass-produced artefacts. But each one is individual, so they can also be regarded as craft objects that are explorations of materials modelled by hand. In New York (where he has lived since 1980) and since 2004 in Milan, Pesce's

furniture and objects are made by his own company Fish Design, and in Italy production is managed by Zerodisegno. The 543 Broadway chair (1993), named after the address of his New York studio, is made in larger numbers by Bernini and is the most commercial of his designs, but typically each chair is individual.

Nobody's Perfect sideboard, manufactured by Zerodisegno, Italy, 2002. Polyurethane resin, nylon pins. Photo: courtesy of zerodisegno.

543 Broadway chair, manufactured by Bernini, Italy, 1993. Resin, stainless steel, nylon. Photo: courtesy of Bernini.

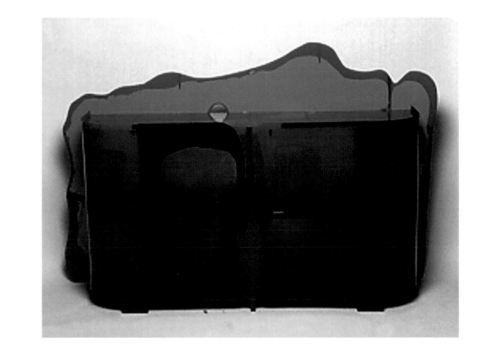

La Smorfia chair, manufactured by Meritalia, Italy, 2003. Closed-cell semi-expanded PVC, polyurethane foam, steel. Photo: courtesy of Meritalia.

Chapter Five

Design Manifestos

S(h)it on It bench, designed by
Richard Hutten, manufactured
by Droog Design, the Netherlands,
1994. Steel, varnished MDF.
Collection Droog Design. Photo:
courtesy of Droog Design.

The most startling and confrontational recent
furniture has come from designers working
on the margins of industrial design, where
their practice merges with conceptual and
installation art. They are less concerned with
functionalism, fashion, or mass production
than many of the designers examined so far,
and their work is seldom intended to please
the mass market. If anything, they make
furniture-shaped political or social manifestos:
agenda-laden signs that exist primarily to
think about rather than use. Often these are
unique objects, or made in very small batches,
and they always have strong visual impact.
This is design for the age of mass media:
we don't need to buy it but we know about it
from the internet, television, style magazines
or books.

Broadly speaking, this chapter is about
conceptual designers: designers who value
ideas above technique, or style, or function.
If twentieth-century design was dominated
by rationalism, then these designers seem to
be suggesting that twenty-first century design
will be about emotions and symbolism. They
often use archetypes to conjure up feelings
of nostalgia, or to symbolize enduring values.
Unlike Pop designers, who were preoccupied
with predicting the future, these are designers
who feel continuity with the past.

In the early 1990s Richard Hutten
(a graduate of the Design Academy in Eindhoven and an early member of Droog Design)
designed furniture based on an archetype.
He chose the most simplified and instantly
identifiable type of table, and reduced it to

Baghdad table, designed by
Ezri Tarazi, manufactured
by Edra, 2005. Extruded
aluminium sections.
Photo: courtesy of Edra.

just three primary elements: a top, four rails
to support it and a leg at each corner. Dutch
designer and editor Ed van Hinte observed
this was in fact the symbol of a table, since
a symbol is a common form that collectively
we recognize.[1] Regardless of distortions in
scale we will always mentally configure these
components as a table. By working with an
archetype Hutten sought to erase the presence
of the designer, a process he described as 'no
sign of design'. 'With these elements Richard
Hutten does not strive for minimization of
matter, but for optimization of both function
and meaning,' wrote Van Hinte. 'In this way
he extends the definition of functionalism
from the technical "ability to perform"
by adding "the ability to be clearly understood".'[2] So the archetypal table formula liberated Hutten to make other furniture hybrids
that were equally clearly understood, none

less so than his iconic S(h)it on It bench
(1994). Shaped like a swastika, it forced
the four occupants to sit with their backs to
one another. This bench, much publicized,
demonstrated the emotive power of furniture
that had been refined to its most symbolic
level, even if the symbols (a table, a Nazi
sign) were unconnected.

Richard Hutten showed that a defiant
anti-fascist statement could be made through
the relatively anodyne medium of seating,
and a visitor to an exhibition in Bremen
agreed with him, scratching the words '*Nie
Wieder*' (never again) into the bench. But is
furniture really capable of communicating
political points of view? A decade or so later,
when international attention was focused on
the legitimacy of the Iraq War, Ezri Tarazi
responded with tables, made from sections
of aluminium extrusions, that were maps of

Smoke armchair and chandelier,
designed by Maarten Baas,
2002, manufactured by Moooi,
2004. Burnt wood preserved
in clear epoxy, leather upholstery.
Photo: Maarten van Houten.

Baghdad based on aerial photographs of the
Iraqi capital broadcast globally on television
during the US and UK invasion in 2003.
That Tarazi is the Director of the Industrial
Design Department at the Bezalel Academy
of Art and Design in Jerusalem, and Israel is
an ally of the invaders, lent distinct ambiguity
to any political commentary that the tables
may have embodied. The lattice-like table-
tops were so open as to render them fairly
useless, and their function as tables was
almost entirely incidental to their role as
conceptual art. Yet they were exhibited
by Edra at the Milan Furniture Fair in 2005
and they could, presumably, be ordered
as furniture items.

Two years earlier Maarten Baas first
showed his Smoke furniture in Milan at
the time that Baghdad fell to the Americans.
With serendipity rather than intent his
burnt furniture could have been dragged from
the opulent but charred interiors of Saddam
Hussein's palaces, and they too assumed the
role of commentators on grave world events.
Daniel Charny's Global (2002) was a standard
geographic globe where the countries and
national boundaries had been blacked out.
Charny, a friend of Tarazi, is an Israeli
designer who leads a platform on the Design
Products course at the Royal College of
Art. A prototype of his blackened globe
was shown at the Milan Furniture Fair by
Hidden, a short-lived but forward-thinking
and conceptually inclined Dutch manufacturer
for which Ron Arad was Creative Director
for a time. Global functioned dually as a playful three-dimensional noticeboard for chalk
messages, and as a dark personal commentary
on the state of global politics. Furniture,
therefore, may always need to remain broadly
functional, but it can still be the conveyor of
incisive social messages, much like literature,
art or avant-garde fashion. 'Why doesn't
furniture show that everything is a political
choice?' asked Philippe Starck, who designed
lamps with bases that looked like gilded
AK-47s and black shades lined with crosses
(2005). 'I am a designer and design is my
only weapon, so I use it to speak about what
I think is important.' However, Starck's
rifles-to-lighting concept was no swords-
to-ploughshares design epiphany. They said
nothing about war or peace, and were just
kitsch home accessories for the 'bling-bling'
generation.[3] Perhaps this was his point.
'We kill out of ambition, out of greed, for the
fun of it or for the show,' wrote Starck, declar-
ing that weapons are society's new icons.
'The Guns collection is nothing but a sign

Faraday chair, designed by
Dunne & Raby, 1995. Acrylic,
steel, silicon, cotton. V&A:
W.674-2001, given by
Dunne & Raby.

of the times. We get the symbols we deserve.'⁴
If Starck is right and we get the symbols
we deserve, what are we to make of the
Faraday chair, an early work by Anthony
Dunne and Fiona Raby (1995)? This took the
form of a tank that symbolically shielded its
user from bombardment by invisible radiation
emitted by electrical appliances, and was
named after Michael Faraday (1791-1867),
a pioneering researcher into electricity. In no
way did the Faraday chair actually function,
other than symbolically. Much work by Dunne
& Raby concerns itself with protection from
the effects of technology, and the Faraday
chair eloquently symbolized the fact that these
effects might not always be benign. 'Like all
chairs it is an echo of the human body and
communicates a new image of technoman,'
they wrote.'Not a cyborg fusing with technology, nor a master of technology, but one
of vulnerability and uncertainty about the
long-term effects of the technological space
we have so enthusiastically constructed.'⁵

Micro-architecture like this tank could
become necessities in the future, they were
suggesting, as the pace of technological
development outstrips our human abilities
to cope with it. Seen like this, the Faraday
chair also evokes the alienation and anxiety
of the individual in modern life, which are
concerns more usually addressed by artists
than by furniture designers. Like art, it
is a unique and complex object that needs
decoding. While Starck designed products
to provoke and shock us, Dunne & Raby,
perhaps more than any other designers
of the period, invited us to think.

The brothers Humberto and Fernando
Campana are based in Sao Paolo, Brazil, one
of the most populous cities on Earth, and much
of their furniture evokes the lives of people
living in the *favelas*, the shanty towns that
are a familiar feature of South American
urban life. The Campanas design furniture
that draws attention to the gulf between the
rich and the poor. They use the same poor

materials – wood off-cuts, rags, plastic tube or corrugated cardboard – as furniture-makers in the *favelas*, who use any and every resource available. Whereas Dunne & Raby hint at a sinister, anxious world, the Campanas' furniture is only a joyous celebration of human achievements over adversity, with no reference to or inference of the pernicious grinding realities that accompany extreme poverty. More often than not they are more interested in the materials and techniques used in the *favelas* than in addressing the social or political realities of the shanties. Their Favela armchair was made of wood off-cuts, but aside from its name it made little other reference to these marginal communities, and in December 2004 the brothers used the same technique to make a Favela mural in Murray Moss's upscale Manhattan design gallery. Without a trace of irony, the Campanas' work is presented to the international design fraternity by Edra, the most avant-garde of the Italian luxury furniture manufacturers. The Campanas' commitment to popularizing issues of poverty in South America is genuine, but their work seems to lack critical clarity. Could they be only exploiting the style of the *favelas* for the sake of fashion (a kind of 'Mardi Gras chic')? Tord Boontje has also worked with the people of the *favelas*, designing lighting that employed their craft skills, in a process that seemed more symbiotic.[6] That the Campanas are Brazilian and Boontje was a European outsider must also be considered in the relationship of designers to local communities and issues.

Several designers have sought to combine First World design nous and Third World hand skills, often as a means of benefiting the latter. These projects have a political agenda and a strong ethical commitment too; they are design manifestos for a better world. Often they are more like practical applications of skills and technologies than essays in conceptual theory. One such project organized by

Dutch designer Piek Suyling sought to match the craft skills of Indian and Moroccan artisans with aluminium shelving components made industrially in Europe. Called Cabinets of Cultures, Suyling's project uncomfortably married the partners, with the Third World decoration looking like an appendage to the modern furniture. Despite its failings the experiment itself was very valid since it used design as a means to effect social and economic change for the better.[7] Another example of socially orientated furniture production was Illizi Home, an employment creation programme set up by BP in Algeria in 2001, later gaining the support of the UK Department for International Development, and named after a town in the south of the country. Although it would be easy to regard the project cynically as a sweetener for BP's North African oil exploration, by 2005 some 700 Algerian artisans were employed making furniture, ceramics, baskets and rugs. Simon Pengelly, Michael Sodeau and Kate Blee all contributed designs and expertise to the project because, according to Sodeau,

Sushi chair, designed by Humberto and Fernando Campana, manufactured by Edra, Italy, 2002. Various fabrics, polyurethane and fabric tube. Photo: courtesy of Edra.

Favela chair, designed by Humberto and Fernando Campana, manufactured by Edra, Italy 2003. Untreated wood. Photo: courtesy of Edra

the involvement of British designers ensured the designs were palatable to the international market and so could achieve a higher purchase price for the Algerian manufacturers. Illizi Home supported Algerian artisans with education programmes to revitalize craft skills, and provided purely practical things such as air conditioning and a dyeing plant for yarns. Perhaps ironically the Algerian government did not financially support the initiative for the reason that the products were not distinctly Algerian, and Illizi Home had to work hard to persuade Algerian craftspeople to work within an international design vocabulary, thereby making it internationally competitive. The Algerian carpet-weavers needed to be re-educated in vegetable dyeing, as the Western market prefers the irregularities of this to the flatness of synthetic dyes. Conversely the furniture makers thought Pengelly's furniture was too simple as it lacked ornamentation. Arguably the Illizi Home product range, particularly the furniture, was non-specifically international and bland, rather than imbued with local style, but this was a hard-headed decision to make it as appealing to the market as possible. Illizi Home could become sustainable without institutional or governmental grants in five or ten years. This was design and production with a concept of social and economic development at its heart. It made more than just media-friendly provocative statements about issues and appeared to be sustainable in the long term.[8]

For a period in the mid-1990s design debates were dominated by the concept of sustainability, whether through environmentally friendly manufacturing processes and materials, through recycling, or through extending the lifespan of objects. To an extent these issues dimmed as the decade progressed but arguably this was because sustainable practices such as recycling became mainstream. Theorists expounded on ideas of longevity, whereby objects were suffused with character or were hardwired into our emotions, meaning we were supposedly less likely to discard them in favour of new models. Jurgen Bey's Light Shade shade – a cover to disguise your out-of-fashion lamp to which you are nostalgically attached – was the prime example of this 'added value' design concept (see page 37).

The Netherlands Design Institute, headed by John Thackara, debated sustainability and longevity, and begat the Eternally Yours Foundation that itself generated two influential volumes of essays in 1997 and 2004.[9] A general response to our society's

wasteful use of resources was to short-circuit the fashionability of new objects, in part by appropriating past styles or archetypes. As we have seen in earlier chapters, appropriating design motifs and simplifying design languages go hand in hand and are attempts to find simple, timeless standards of design. Anne Marchand concluded that, conceptually, a simple object is 'an idea whose implications include both the notion of archetype and a reduction in technical complexity.'[10] This could certainly describe the bench Jurgen Bey presented as part of the Droog Design project 'Couleur Locale' in 1999. He stripped the idea of what furniture is right back to its most elemental nature – the wood from which much of it is made – and only added casts of existing Victorian chair backs to the hewn log to indicate and signify its transformation (see page 38). Nature and culture were cross-fertilized. The light touch of a gifted designer, or an example of the Emperor's New Clothes depending on your point of view, Bey's bench questioned what is appropriate and necessary in design. The archetype he evoked was a rustic, arcadian, simplified, naive ideal.[11] Jasper Morrison and the New Functionalists had also experimented with archetypes, but for them purity of form was a means of achieving the best functionality. Hutten and Bey were seeking the most expressive design language and issues of comfort or use were more or less immaterial. By appropriating old Victorian furniture

Loop collection, designed by Simon Pengelly, manufactured by Illizi Home, Algeria, 2005. Walnut, wool and foam upholstery. Photo: courtesy of Illizi Home.

for the seatbacks on the bench, and as he did again with the St Petersburg Chair in 2003, Bey played with our associations of previously fashionable styles. Bey particularly likes the bourgeois connotations of late-Victorian parlour style and subversions of it appear frequently in his work, as they do in the work of Maarten Baas, his pupil at the Design Academy in Eindhoven. It was, therefore, no stylistic coincidence that Baas's first piece of Smoke furniture was a burnt Victorian rococo revival chair.

Designers used archetypes because of the symbolic value derived from their standardized forms. Conversely, they also sought to personalize their furniture in order to individualize it. Conceptually led designers saw the value in customizing their objects so each one was different, perhaps by allowing haphazard factors to affect the production, just as Gaetano Pesce had explored random effects in his resin and plastic objects. Aside from creating more interesting production runs, Pesce believed that individualizing

products invested them with character. Quasi-mystically he concluded that 'character' equates to 'soul': 'Objects as well have the right to be similar to one another, like individuals. Similar, not identical.' Self-evidently he was wrong, as an insensate object cannot have rights (or it would be an animate subject), but by 'liberating objects from their slavery and going beyond the idea of standardization', Pesce was really exploring how people relate to the artefacts they use.[12] For Pesce and many other designers, individualizing objects and imbuing them with a sense of personality were key to enabling users to build personal, lasting relationships with them.

A group of young Swedish designers calling themselves Front explored the way in which random factors could contribute character to designed objects. They were interested to discover what would happen if they let someone, or something, else determine an aspect of the design. Included in their 'Design by Animals' collection (2003) was a roll of wallpaper that had been gnawed

St Petersburg chair, designed by Jurgen Bey, manufactured by Droog Design, the Netherlands, 2003. Existing chair, PVC foam, glass reinforced polyester, silk screen decoration. Collection Droog Design. Photo: courtesy of Droog Design.

Table by insects, from the 'Design by Animals' collection, designed by Front, prototype, Sweden, 2003. Wood. Photo: Anna Lönnerstam.

St Petersburg chair, designed by Jurgen Bey, manufactured by Droog

by a rat. Once hung on the wall, the rat's contribution would add an uneven yet decorative pattern to the uniform, industrially produced wallpaper. This is similar, yet fundamentally different, to the Peep Show wallpaper designed by Gijs Bakker for Droog Design (1992). Here, circular holes pierced the paper in a regular pattern, revealing and framing portions of the old wallpaper beneath, to enhance its nostalgic value. 'The look is determined less by the wallpaper itself than by the wall underneath, retaining a link with the past,' he wrote.[13] Other prototypes by Front included vases cast from the shapes left by dogs' legs in deep snow and a wooden table decorated with the radiating patterns made by certain wood-boring larvae. The last example reveals the contradictory nature of Front's concept because the pattern was not actually made by the larvae on the table, but scanned from an example in nature and artificially applied. Despite the name of the collection, animals do not in fact design in the same way that people design, or for the same ends. Despite their aim, Front retained control of any design decisions because the animals themselves were not consciously designing anything, they were merely behaving. Furthermore, the results may have looked like quirky prototypes of customized products, but actually they performed as little more than three-dimensional calling cards for Front's talents as industrial

Photograph by Bianca Pilet of Do Add #1 chair, designed by Jurgen Bey for the Droog Design and Kesselskramer Do Create project, 2000. Laminate and chromium-plated steel.

Photograph by Bianca Pilet of Do Hit, designed by Marijn van der Poll for the Droog Design and Kesselskramer Do Create project, 2000. Stainless steel, hammer.

designers. As recent graduates must do everywhere, the members of Front used their design ideas as a form of public relations to get themselves noticed. In their case, it worked and within two years of graduating the group was being fêted in London, Milan and elsewhere.[14] This does not invalidate the originality of their ideas in themselves, but shows how conceptual design and successful marketing strategies can become blurred.

In a project conducted with the Amsterdam advertising agency Kesselskramer, Droog Design explored how the design of objects could be completed by interaction with their users. In the prevailing spirit of enhancing and prolonging our relationships with our consumer products, it was about what people might do to things to make them their own. The project, called 'Do Create', had clear benefits for both instigators. For the Droog

designers it was an opportunity to explore the intimate relationships of people to things without the imperative of designing commercially viable products. For its part, Kesselskramer stood to gain credibility as a cutting-edge agency in tune with the latest design ideas. Their contribution was the somewhat woolly notion of 'doing' as 'a brand that is open to ideas from anyone and anywhere… As an ever-changing brand, do is, by definition, always unfinished. Do products or services or events can only exist with the interaction of consumers, brands and others who want to do.'[15] To a significant degree, therefore, Do Create was another example of conceptual design being co-opted as a marketing strategy, underlined by the fact that Do Create existed primarily as a set of widely published, staged photographs by Bianca Pilet showing 'ordinary' people

127

interacting with the products. That aside, the project included furniture and objects by a roll call of the international avant-garde, including Martí Guixé (Spain), Radi Designers (France), Thomas Bernstrand (Sweden) and Dick van Hoff, Frank Tjepkema and Jurgen Bey (all from the Netherlands). All the products demanded physical contact: cutting, smashing, hanging, scratching, connecting or balancing. Bey made a series of chairs called Do Add with legs of unequal length, or other imbalances that needed to be countered. Do Hit was Marijn van der Poll's steel box that was supplied with a hammer. 'Hit, smash and bash to your heart's content and sculpt for yourself the shape you want it to be. Make it shallow, make it deep, the choice is up to you. Suddenly, after a few minutes or a few hours of work, you'll have become the co-designer of "do hit", with the bonus of enjoying, or suffering, a healthy bout of exercise.'[16] All this effort to make a vague and ugly approximation of an early Ron Arad beaten steel chair! In one important respect the Do Create concept overlooked most peoples' commonplace experience of furniture, which was the self-assembly of flat-packs from stores such as IKEA. We were already intimately interacting with the making of our furniture. The difference with Do Create was that users could influence the outcome much more directly than they could with a Pax wardrobe or a Billy bookcase.[17]

'Manolo is gonna have fun' was a conceptual collection by two Spanish designers living in London, Héctor Serrano and Lola Llorca, presented at Designers Block in 2001 and in Milan the following year. Serrano, a graduate of the Design Products course at the Royal College of Art, had won the Peugeot Design Award in 2000 with his Superpatata lamp, a gel-filled and pliable, illuminated orb that Droog Design incorporated into its collection. The underlying concept of the new collection was that fun could be built into everyday objects and activities, and to unite the disparate designs Serrano and Llorca invented Manolo. 'Who is Manolo?' they asked. 'Manolo is a character. He works as an administrator for the government. He is a serious man with traditional values. Manolo doesn't go out too much. He prefers to stay at home. But he has left his city to travel to London and participate in Manolo's gonna have fun exhibition.'[18] The brochure that accompanied the collection included photographs by Jordi A. Tomàs of a stout and stoic moustachioed Spaniard (Manolo, modelled by Jose Manual Domingo) undertaking

Photograph by Jordi A. Tomàs of trampoline table designed by Héctor Serrano and Lola Llorca for the 'Manolo is gonna have fun' collection, 2001.

extraordinary activities in the very ordinary environs of London streets and parks. In one picture, the tablecloth of his coffee table revealed itself to be the top of a trampoline. Another photograph showed him kicking a large inflatable object along the street: the caption instructs us to 'simply use like a normal lamp football'. All the objects were humorous takes on familiar domestic items and required the user's complicity. They were not objects of contemplation but of action. Yet, on another level, they were purely objects of contemplation because, like the Do Create collection, they existed principally as prototypes made to furnish photographic images. The designer's ideas were communicated, not through the production and sale of the objects themselves, but through their presentation in the media.

We see a pattern emerging of conceptual designs presented as one-off objects within the frameworks of stories or narratives constructed for the media. They are seldom prototypes awaiting the attentions of manufacturers, or finished products to be bought and used (and as such they are the 'unpasteurized' design visions so admired by Murray Moss in the introduction to this book). The concept underlying the design process is most important, not the realization of the furniture in the market-place. The designers' ideas are communicated through the pictures, not through production of the objects themselves. In a sense this is similar to the way high fashion is consumed; advertisements and the fashion press inspire aspiration, but few people will ever wear it. Consumers experience the image, not the actual object. Complete product stories, like that which Héctor Serrano and Lola Llorca imagined for Manolo, are seductive tales, but the furniture has little actual relevance because it remains fictional. Conceptual design, therefore, can sometimes be merely a witty idea dressed up as clever social commentary or philosophical musing when it is neither. More often, as has been shown in this chapter, it is an exercise in public relations and it shows the way that furniture design has become part of the media and fashion-driven 'lifestyle industry', which is the subject of the last chapter in this book.

Designers use narratives to frame their ideas, whether they are geo-political allusions (Tarazi's Baghdad table), overt works of fiction (Manolo) or concepts (such as 'nostalgia' and 'longevity', on which Jurgen Bey grounds his furniture). The French designer Matali Crasset uses narrative in a different way, as the design process itself. For her, story-telling and imagined scenarios underlie everything she designs: she creates stories that are design problems, then creates objects that are their solutions. For example, she asked what would happen when her cousin Jim visited her in Paris. Her small apartment had no spare bedroom and sofa-beds are clumsy

'When Jim Comes to Paris' hospitality tower, designed by Matali Crasset, manufactured by Domeau & Pérès, France, 1995. Polyurethane foam, felt, cotton, electrical fittings. Photo: Patrick Gries.

Bookworm bookshelf, designed
by Ron Arad, manufactured by
Kartell, Italy, 1994. PVC. V&A:
W.2-1996, given by Kartell.

and uncomfortable, she concluded, yet Jim would need somewhere to sleep. He would need a bedside lamp, too, and a clock to wake him in the morning. These constraints and requirements generated a design that was a new paradigm of what a spare bed could be: a bed-roll stored vertically inside a padded 'hospitality tower' that unfolded to make the bed base. A lamp and a clock simply hooked on to the tower, which had a far smaller footprint than any other folding bed when not in use. Crasset had worked with Philippe Starck at TimThom, the research studio for Thomson, between 1994 and 1997. Like Starck, she has a gift for naivety and for thinking about the world in a childlike way, and much of her furniture engages the imagination of children. Her Oritapi carpet (1999), for example, transformed into a play house, and her Licence to Build modular sofa (2000) was nothing more than an assemblage of outsized soft building bricks. Underlying all her designs is the question 'What if....?', and her objects are often part of a larger narrative process. They seem to have grown directly from the cartoon strip drawings she makes.[19] Similarly, furniture by Ineke Hans, another designer in tune with her inner child, often has a fairytale quality to it. Neither designer intends her work to exist only as prototypes, media images, or unique pieces in museums. Their narrative, conceptual approach is intended to take their work into production. The small Parisian firm of Domeau and Pérès made Crasset's furniture described here, but in small editions and with limited distribution. Few, if any, of Ineke Hans's designs are mainstream mass-produced products. Ideas-led furniture design will almost always only command a limited market.

On occasion, however, a left-field concept can become a commercial success, and one such was Ron Arad's Bookworm bookshelf – a best-selling product for Kartell since its introduction in 1994. Unlike most industrial products its shape was not permanently fixed during production. There were factors that controlled the design, such as the degree of flexibility of the extruded PVC and the regular positioning along its length of the wall-fixings, but ultimately the look and usefulness of the book shelf derived from the way it was hung by the person who would use it. Like the Do Hit chair, or Tokujin Yoshioka's Honey-Pop chair, the user became the 'co-designer'. This was a random factor beyond the control of Arad or Kartell and a different arbitrary quality from that examined in the

work of Pesce in the previous chapter. In those works, the random act took place during production. The new concept with the Bookworm was that it was personalized in use, not during manufacture. More than with most furniture, the user was intimately and physically engaged with determining the formation of the Bookworm, and one might argue that this interaction with the furniture engages the user in a more direct and personal way than is conventional. Moreover, the Bookworm, which began life as a mild steel one-off, then a standardized and neutral plastic extrusion, had to be personalized, because it could only function after there had been individual interaction with the end user. The Bookworm stands to one side of most of the furniture discussed in this chapter simply by virtue of its commercial success. As concepts go, Arad's was a winner. It marked the moment when Arad, in Deyan Sudjic's words, moved from 'couture to ready-to-wear', by designing an object for volume production and (relatively) mass consumption.[20]

Another designer who converted conceptual design into commercial capital was Marcel Wanders in his role as art director of Moooi (the name derived from the Dutch word for 'beautiful' with an extra 'o' to make it more beautiful!). His dry wit permeates the company's collections, and many of the products are commercially manufactured runs based on unique one-offs, where the form and message have been standardized but retain their impact (just as Kartell interpreted Arad's original metal Bookworm shelf in plastic). Jurgen Bey's Light Shade shade, for example, enclosed a modern chandelier, not a family heirloom (see page 37). Maarten Baas's Smoke furniture was serially produced. Several arms of his original chandelier had burnt away entirely, a flaw faithfully reproduced in Moooi's production version. Constantin and Laurene Leon Boym contributed Salvation Ceramics, which were stacks of rejected or cast-off porcelain tableware bonded into new decorative objects. Moooi, therefore, succeeded in popularizing the ironic and nostalgic conceptual designs associated with Droog Design on a scale that had always eluded Droog itself.

Wanders' interest in the longevity of objects inspired him to design a collection of 'new antiques' for Cappellini (2005) that looked like ebonized Victorian turned-wood furniture. Stylistically they were only a step away from being reproduction furniture (and many manufacturers of reproduction styles would have made a better job of it). In the same year Wanders pursued the idea with tables and desks for Moooi that looked like old furniture. In the market, the only thing that separated these from actual reproduction antique furniture was Wanders' ironic presentation of the objects, and the savvy customers' knowledge of his irony. The 'new antiques' idea, although based on design theories developed by Wanders and many others over more than a decade, looked like a tired - but commercially sound - concept.

It seems that designers of conceptual furniture can generally only thrive as part of the media, at the fashionable margins of the commercial market, or in the art market. Increasingly unique pieces by conceptual designers are finding their way into the modern art market, through the auction houses and a select number of dealers. Like artworks, they are unique or from numbered, signed editions, and they are laden with symbolic meaning. The advantage to designers of being regarded as artists is principally pecuniary, as the art market offers far greater financial rewards than the more limited ghettoized markets for craft or designer-makers' works. The art market is bigger, richer and more developed. Considered as art, the furniture is absolved from any presumption of function, enabling the designers to pursue purely conceptual ends for their work. And on a purely practical level, the art market is an outlet for designers to offload and cash in their works once the projects or commissions that instigated them are completed.

Conceptual design has become a provocative and fertile area of furniture design since 1990. Whereas design debates were previously dominated by Italian designers, increasingly they have become centred on the Netherlands, but by no means exclusively. A challenge to designers has been how to commercialize their ideas without diluting them, and how to harness media channels without becoming hijacked by them. Conceptual furniture designers have achieved both by positioning themselves in the vanguard of fashion, and the effect of 'lifestyle' and the fashion system on furniture is the subject of the last chapter.

New Antiques collection, designed
by Marcel Wanders, manufactured
by Cappellini, Italy, 2005. Turned
and lacquered wood, polyurethane
foam, leather, glass. Photo: courtesy
of Cappellini.

Droog Design

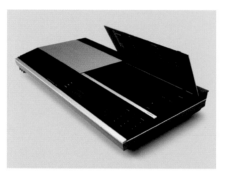

Since 1993 Droog Design has created its own place in design culture because uniquely it combines the functions of a PR company, a manufacturer, a gallery, a design collective and a philosophy. Aaron Betsky defines Droog Design as 'a seal of approval', indicating that it is, in fact, a brand.[1] At the heart of its activities is a collection of objects edited and compiled by the art historian Renny Ramakers and the designer and educator Gijs Bakker, both of whom are Dutch. At the beginning of the 1990s they perceived a new spirit pervading work by a young generation of Dutch designers that included Richard Hutten, Hella Jongerius, Marcel Wanders and Tejo Remy. Common to all their objects was an ironic, detached, and sometimes whimsical analysis of the rituals of everyday life, giving rise to the Droog name, meaning 'dry' in Dutch. Droog Design introduced a heavily conceptual approach to the design of everyday objects. One recurrent concern was that design today is a response to history, and very many Droog

Design products refer obliquely or overtly to historical archetypes (Jurgen Bey's furniture, for example, or Joris Laarman's rococo concrete radiators, 2003). The designers appear to accommodate and reinterpret history, which often makes them appear at odds with modernity. Another recurrent theme was 'Dutchness' and the symbols of Dutch culture, expressed, for instance, through reinterpretations of Delftware. Most prevalent, however, was the concept of irony, as in Max Wolf, Markus Bader and Sebastian Oschatz's Bootleg objects (2003): reinterpretations of obsolete electrical appliances given contemporary functionality. This also manifested itself as a disregard for commonly held, obvious ideas of what is beautiful, and a relish for more awkward beauties achieved through unexpected juxtapositions of scale, ornament or materials, as in Martí Guixé's outsize Private Rocking Chair (2001) and Hella Jongerius's seemingly contradictory Soft Vase (1995).

Droog Design exists as much as a media and publishing event as it does an actual collection of objects to purchase, and it has struggled to market its products commercially. Annual fringe exhibitions at the Milan Furniture Fair secured their place in the avant-garde. They were often themed or were the result of collaborations with manufacturers and partners, including Rosenthal, and the German city of Oranienbaum. For one memorable exhibition in 2002 Droog Design occupied a low-rent Milanese hotel, inserting discrete products into the austere and shabby bedrooms: Joost Grootens' sinister bulletproof sleeping bag lay across one bed. The objects in the collections and their stylish and provocative presentation became intertwined, and they are as much works of conceptual art as they are prototypes of actual products for the market-place.

From the outset Droog Design, laden with irony, attitude, quirkiness and intelligence, ran counter to minimalism. The difference between the prevailing Italian design thinking and the new Dutch approach was that in Italy craftsmanship, beauty and symbolism were revered, whereas arguably the Dutch designers invited accidental effects and accommodated humour too. Their conceptual approach was quickly emulated outside the Netherlands, especially in Britain, Spain and Scandinavia, and increasingly the Droog Design collections included non-Dutch

Cow chair, designed by Neils van Eijk, 1997. Cow hide. Collection Droog Design. Photo: Marsel Loermans.

designers such as Hector Serrano and Noriko Yasuda.

An early Droog Design publication was titled 'Spirit of the Nineties', and in a very real way the group can lay claim to the dominant design thinking since 1990. Most influential in schools of design, Droog Design products have only ever reached an elite collectors' market, with the exception being the furniture and products produced commercially by Moooi, the Dutch manufacturer art-directed by Marcel Wanders.

Bullet-proof sleeping bag, designed by Joost Grootens for the Hotel Droog exhibition, Milan, April 2002. Kevlar, embroidery. Collection Droog Design. Photo: courtesy of Droog Design.

Dunne & Raby

'We live in incredibly bland times. I'm shocked at how people are so narrow in the way they think about how you might use objects or space.' [1]

Fiona Raby

Reserved bench, Cucumber Sandwiches table, Talking Tab label tabs, from the Weeds, Aliens and Other Stories collection, designed with Michael Anastassiades, 1998. Oak, glass. V&A: W.70, 75, 76, 77, 78-2002.

Anthony Dunne and Fiona Raby are not furniture designers but many of their objects look like furniture, and are important catalysts in reconsidering what furniture can be like. Since the mid-1990s they have emerged as some of the most original thinkers in British design, embodying their sometimes far-fetched theories into a series of objects and collections that have been widely exhibited and published. As teachers they have inclined a new generation of designers to think conceptually. In 1994 they were founder-members of the Computer-Related Design Research Studio at the Royal College of Art (until 2002) and now they lead studios in the Design Products and Architecture & Interiors departments there. For Dunne & Raby design is a form of ongoing research, a project that is not intended to produce objects for mass-production.

Dunne & Raby do not accept that objects, furniture or appliances have to look or perform as they do. They are chiefly concerned with questioning how people relate to each other and to the modern world, and the role of design as a conduit. For example, the Weeds,

Aliens and Other Stories collection (1998, designed with Michael Anastassiades) explored the emotional bond of people to their gardens as a metaphor for the psychological terrain of interpersonal relationships. This was 'design noir', a term Dunne & Raby invented to describe design that explored issues of alienation and existential angst.

The Placebo collection (2000) was a series of furniture objects that, in different ways, drew attention to the invisible microwaves emitted by familiar appliances such as televisions, computers and telephones. Some of the devices physically responded to electrical stimulation, such as the compasses embedded in a table-top that could detect the presence of a mobile phone. Others were more literally placebos, with psychological and symbolic meanings but no practical functions, such as the electro-draught excluder that did not actually absorb radiation. Dunne & Raby wanted to see if it comforted users to feel they were protected by it. [2] Because it is the purpose, not the appearance, of things that interests Dunne & Raby, many of their designs are for schematized, diagrammatic objects. Visually these are often in tune with the spare functionalist design that was dominant in the 1990s, but they are not really part of the same trend.

'Design for Fragile Personalities in Anxious Times' (2004), another collaboration with Michael Anastassiades, developed the darker aspects of their research. For this project they made human-sized boxes that appeared to grow from parquet flooring and were like panic rooms to flee to in emergencies.

Design needs people like Dunne & Raby who stand outside but comment on it. They are provocative because they make us think in different ways. More specifically, furniture designers can learn from their strange, hybrid, archetypal objects how to reconsider what is appropriate or possible.

Electro-draught excluder from the Placebo project, 2000. MDF, electrically conductive foam, stainless steel. Photo: Jason Evans.

Compass table from the Placebo project, 2000. MDF, compasses. Photo: Jason Evans.

Hide Away furniture from the Design for Fragile Personalities in Anxious Times project, 2004, designed with Michael Anastassiades. Oak and felt. Photo: Jason Evans.

*Wallpaper**, launch issue, September/October 1996.

Chapter Six

Furniture and the Lifestyle Industry

'Design has turned into a tool of fame; designers have become world stars and gurus… Fashion, hype and meaningless trends have invaded the design worlds, and chairs now date more quickly than hemlines… What gets into the news is constant change, the creation of new trends. What is painful about this fashion cycle is the way in which ideas are at first scorned, then adored, then misused and finally rejected, whatever their value.' [1]

Andrée Putman

Today, more than ever, furniture design acts like fashion design, and together they are part of the global lifestyle industry.[2] When writing her introduction to *The International Design Yearbook* in 1992, the French architect and designer Andrée Putman could not conceal her dismay. In this book I have charted many trends since 1990, mostly from the point of view of the designers or the manufacturers. From minimalism to Blobjects and even 'new antiques', we have seen how design ideas, as Putnam says, 'are at first scorned, then adored, then misused and finally rejected, whatever their value'. This chapter explores how the market for contemporary furniture has changed since 1990 and the effect the lifestyle industry has had on it. When did contemporary design become so popular?

The media, of course, is chiefly to blame for the popularizing of design. Publications such as *Homes and Gardens*, published since 1923, had popularized furniture, interiors and 'homemaking' for a mass audience they shared with the Ideal Home exhibitions (dating back to 1908), while women's fashion glossies such as *Vogue* would feature, from the 1920s on, the more glamorous homes of society hostesses as the context for the clothes. Colour supplements, introduced into Sunday newspapers in the 1960s, reached a broad audience and often included features about celebrities' homes or fashionable and innovative design. Furniture design may have been celebrated in these magazines but it was seldom critiqued beyond the trade and architectural press. Magazines such as *Blueprint* (founded in 1983) raised the ante but still had limited circulation beyond designers and architects. First *Elle Decoration* and then *Wallpaper** (launched in 1989 and 1996 respectively) reinterpreted contemporary interiors and furniture in the mass media. The first *Elle Decoration* featured André Dubreuil's home on the cover and its editorial summed up the magazine's approach. 'Style-wise, street-wise and pound-wise, *Elle Decoration* brings the allure of *Elle* to your home. In each issue we feature the up-to-the-minute interiors of the hip and rich, and show you, in wonderful photographs, how to pick up some of their ideas.'[3] It was cool to know the names of furniture designers, especially the Scandinavian and mid-twentieth-century designers. *Wallpaper** (subtitled 'the stuff that surrounds you') had an arch tone and purely aspirational outlook that made it the paradigm of lifestyle magazines of the 1990s, emulated in the US by *Surface*, published in San Francisco. Often it was impossible to tell whether editorial pages were about the clothes worn by the models, the furniture they sat on, or both. Importantly, furniture and fashion were increasingly presented in the same way, and just as fashion magazines celebrate the work of a small band of elite labels (not inconsequentially often their major advertisers), so a handful of media-friendly

wallpaper*

*The stuff that surrounds you

sept | oct 1996
launch issue

urban
Modernists

£3.00 UK

ISSN 1364-4475

interiors ✻ entertaining ✻ travel

furniture designers - the Eameses, Arad, Starck - furnished these magazine pages. For example, an issue of the fashion bible *i-D* entitled 'the sitting issue' included an interview with Karim Rashid and a fashion feature where Vitra chairs were credited along with the designers of the clothes.[4]

Savvy furniture companies picked up this trend and their catalogues emulated the production values of fashion magazines. Edra styled itself like Prada or Gucci, and in many ways it is the furniture equivalent of these luxury brands, an impression reinforced by its collaboration with Swarovski on the Diamond sofa, improbably but impressively encrusted with 750,000 crystals. In contrast, Moooi imagery set out to shock, adopting the same tactics Oliviero Toscani used to great effect for Benetton. Erwin Olaf's images of circus freaks and misfits repelled and attracted in equal measure, and the models often quite literally wore the furniture and products. The brand message was clear: difference and individuality are cool.

In the 1950s and 1960s the Eameses, Conrans and Days were the equivalent of celebrity designers, enjoying some media attention for their 'perfect' lifestyles and marriages (in a sense Charles and Ray Eames were presented like Rock Hudson and Doris Day). In the 1990s the focus shifted from a cult of domesticity to a cult of personality and furniture designers were suddenly seen as cool too, even sexy, more like rock stars. Marc Newson, the closest thing to a pin-up in the world of furniture design, modelled Moschino, Thierry Mugler, Issey Miyake and Paco Rabanne for a 1994 *Sunday Times* shoot that cast him as a spaceman alongside his own stellar furniture designs.[5] Later, he appeared to regret it. 'I never went looking for the pop star image, or all those articles. Now I try to do as few as possible, first because it takes up too much time, and secondly because what's more important to me is to be taken seriously as a designer.' This did not prevent him modelling in advertisements for his range of Samsonite luggage, styled as a glamorous

i-D, 219, April 2002.

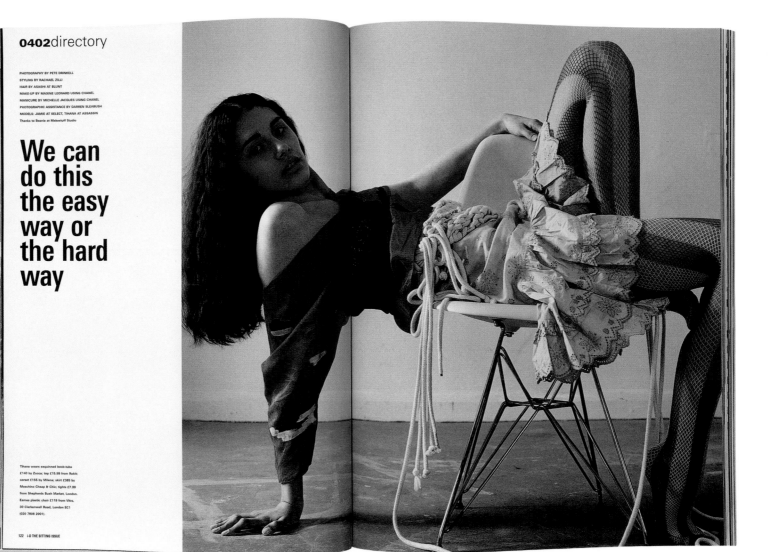

i-D, 219, April 2002.

Diamond sofa, a special edition
Flap sofa, designed by Francesco
Binfare, manufactured by Edra,
Italy, 2001. This version covered
with 750,000 Swarovski crystals.
Photo: courtesy of Edra.

Moooi, promotional photographs
by Erwin Olaf for Light Shade
shade, designed by Jurgen Bey,
1999 and Bottoni sofa, designed
by Marcel Wanders, 2002.

'50's 70's as Today' exhibition of furniture from the Kartell Museum at Dolce & Gabbana, 15 Corso Venezia, Milan, 14–19 April 2004, including furniture by Olaf von Bohr, Achille Castiglioni, Giotto Stoppino, Anna Castelli Ferrieri and Joe Colombo. Photo: courtesy of Kartell.

baggage handler, in 2005.[6] When the Dutch fashion retailer Mexx launched in the UK in 1999, it used the furniture designer Konstantin Grcic to promote its Role Models campaign, under the strap-line 'Real people who are making a difference. Making their mark. Original individuals.' Here, the brand message was that designers are cool.[7]

Furniture companies have adopted the sites of fashion brands and sought the endorsement of fashion designers too. In 2004 30 pieces from the Kartell company archive were exhibited at the time of the Salone del Mobile in the opulent surroundings of the Dolce & Gabbana menswear store in Corso Venezia. 'It was exciting to choose objects from the museum, which we would like to have in our house today,' Domenico Dolce and Stefano Gabbana were quoted as saying. 'Design, style and irony: these are in our opinion the significant and distinctive characteristics that make Kartell and Dolce & Gabbana a perfect team!' In Milan the major site for furniture shows outside the official Salone del Mobile is Superstudio Piu, a vast shed complex ordinarily used to stage catwalk shows during Fashion Week. In 1995 Zerodisegno used the venue for its own catwalk show. Models of both sexes paraded along the runway carrying, and even wearing, the company's products.[8]

At the same venue in 2002 Cappellini dressed its furniture in fabrics by Pucci. Models, in swimming suits to match, lounged on the sofas and divans that appeared to be floating across a swimming pool (the range, called 'Swimming Pool', was by Piero Lissoni). The whole conceit projected fashionable decadence and youthful beauty, arguably the brand values that Cappellini was promoting at the time. Using the fashion system, furniture manufacturers were transforming themselves into lifestyle brands with associated sets of values. And fashion houses responded in kind, launching home furnishing collections that evoked the same values as their clothes and accessories. The launch, in 1983, of Ralph Lauren's country-house style homeware complemented his preppy clothes and is the most famous (and commercially successful) cross-branding by a fashion designer.[9] Versace Home and Fendi featured leather and animal prints on upholstery, while Armani Casa's range was beige and casual like the loosely structured clothes the designer is famed for. Donna Karan entrusted her homeware ranges to Ilse Crawford and Margaret Howell sells vintage Ercol furniture alongside her clothes in her Wigmore Street flagship store. Paul Smith often uses *trompe-l'oeil* prints for his clothes, and his designs for Cappellini's Mondo range in 2002 used enlarged photographic prints (of baroque furniture, for example) to decorate furniture. Smith has friends who are well known for their furniture and he admitted 'I felt that it might be disrespectful to enter their world

Swimming Pool collection, designed by Piero Lissoni, upholstery by Pucci, manufactured by Cappellini, 2002. Photos: courtesy of Cappellini.

Imaginary Discoteca, published
by Tricatel for David Design,
2001, and Cap One, published
by Nuphonic for Cappellini,
2002, music CDs.

as I have no formal training in furniture design. When I finally accepted the commission I thought that my approach should be more as a stylist rather than as a designer.'[10] His reticence was well-founded: his contribution to the three-dimensional forms of the furniture was negligible and only the surface decoration was recognizably his. The French fashion designer Hedi Slimane designs menswear for Christian Dior, but his debut collection of matt-black metal furniture in 2004 was for Comme des Garçons (his own office furniture was designed for him by the Bouroullec brothers). Slimane had engaged more fully in the design process than Smith had, and his furniture was reminiscent of Judd, Rietveld and Richard Hutten too. It was retailed through the Dover Street Market, Rei Kawakubo's London HQ for her global Comme des Garçons fashion empire, where vintage Jean Prouvé furniture was also sold.[11]

So furniture companies have appropriated fashion's imagery, but they have emulated the soundtrack of the catwalk show too. Marcel Wanders and Dutch multimedia artist Ton Driessens produced a CD of experimental, quirky music to accompany the Droog Design exhibition 'Couleur Locale' in Milan in 1999. In Sweden David Design issued *Imaginery Discoteca* (Tricatel, compiled by Olivier Rohrbach, 2001): the sleeve bore the exhortation 'have fun, stay cool' alongside pictures of David Design's products. The music was an eclectic mix of easy-listening European dance-oriented tracks intended to complement the easy-going, modern and relaxed product offering.

Cappellini launched a dance music compilation, *Cap One*, on the Nuphonic label in 2002, featuring international artists that included Röyksopp, Ultra Naté and Nitin Sawhney. The album should be regarded as a musical expression of the company's brand values, while the sleeve notes by Giulio Cappellini read like nothing less than the copy of a Calvin Klein scent advertisement.

> *We like exploring, listening, mixing*
> *and playing.*
> *We like speaking different languages.*
> *We like coherence, and we like*
> *contradiction.*
> *We like traces and hints, not impositions.*
> *We like the plural more than the singular*
> *and we like thinking globally...*
> *We like design, but we also like fashion,*
> *art and music...*
> *We like atmosphere, and we don't*
> *like limitation, border and definition*
> *in style...*
> *We like 'the idea of a home'.*

The language is that of international style marketing designed to appeal to global, fashionable, urban youth, from Tokyo to Reykjavik, just as the music was non-confrontationally and vaguely Balearic and Brazilian. The CD came boxed with a miniature Cappellini catalogue and scale models of furniture including a tiny 'S' chair by Tom Dixon and a self-assembly Sunset chair by Christophe Pillet: furniture design was commodified as a toy.[12]

Another aspect to leak from the fashion industry into furniture design was the forecasting of trends. For the Moooi Weer sub-brand Marcel Wanders invited the fashion forecaster (and head of Design Academy Eindhoven) Li Edelkoort to propose a paint colour each year that Moooi customers could use to revitalize their old furniture. It was the commercialization of ideas by the Eternally Yours Foundation. 'Forecasting the weather in interior design for 2002/03 is not about the dark grey of thunder or the green grey of spring rains nor the pure white of clouds,' she wrote in the Moooi catalogue, 'but about bright sunny spells translated into a vivid yellow paint with a soft finish and a heavy, slick tactility, almost like oil paint. A yellow ray of sun strong enough to shock all greys and beiges into oblivion.'[13] In other years her colours were red or gold. The inclusion of the annual paint colour in the product range reinforced the impression that this furniture company was acting like a fashion

house. It was also a tongue-in-cheek act of rebellion, seemingly undermining its own product range by endorsing make-do-and-mend restoration of old furniture rather than the purchase of something new. In this respect it was similar to the self-conscious posturing and irony of a hip fashion label such as Diesel.

The gloss and seduction of fashion, therefore, infiltrated the contemporary furniture market in many guises and for many reasons. The boundaries around furniture became more porous and contemporary design began to feature across the media. When, at the beginning of the 1990s, property prices in Britain began to soar, the national passion for home improvement became directly linked to the exorbitant cost of home ownership. Our homes were our chief financial investment, burden and liability and must be maintained. For those unable to trade up, interior decoration and modification improved where we lived and added value. Little wonder, then, that contemporary design was fetishized

Landi chair, designed by Hans Coray, 1938, reissued by Zanotta, Italy, 1971, painted with Moooiweer yellow paint by Moooi, The Netherlands, 2002. Painted aluminium. Photo: courtesy of Moooi Weer.

Space, published weekly as
a supplement to the *Guardian*,
UK, 1997–2001.

through television make-over shows and magazines. When, in 1997, the *Guardian* newspaper launched *Space* for circulation within the M25, its weekly property and interiors supplement edited by former *Blueprint* staffer Caroline Roux, it was riding the London property boom. Features on new furniture and home appliances were mingled with property advertisements and critiques of London's 'villages' for potential house-hunters.

The king of home make-over shows, *Changing Rooms*, aired by the BBC from 1996 until 2004, made household names of its interior designer presenters, most notably Laurence Llewellyn Bowen and Linda Barker, and the show both reflected and affected changing national taste. It hitched a tradi-tional masculine passion for DIY to a more feminized interest in interior decoration and its name, with overtones of boutique shopping, suggested the fickleness of fashion. *Changing Rooms* gave us all licence to experiment in the way we furnished our homes. Derided by design critics and designers alike, it appeared to champion kitsch and novelty above genuine design innovation, but its detractors often forgot that the show was entertainment, not education, and seldom took itself too seriously. Nevertheless the ratings success of *Changing Rooms*, and the raft of imitation shows it launched, were indicative of an important shift in the acceptance of contemporary design by the British public. Similarly, the infamous *Big Brother* houses of the notorious Channel 4 reality TV show could be seen as gauges of public taste. At first parsimoniously kitted out by IKEA, the series later had bigger budgets and aspirations that could only be met by Cappellini, Moroso and other top-end Italian design-led furnishers.

Books have also played a significant role in promoting contemporary design, by bring-ing seductive images right into our homes and onto our coffee tables. In 1980 18-year-old Benedikt Taschen opened a shop selling comics in Cologne, but only a decade later Taschen's own publications were popularizing contemporary design worldwide. With huge print-runs and multilingual text in each vol-ume, Taschen could reduce costs, and coupled with the tumbling cost of colour reproduction, his affordable glossy picture books opened up new markets for design. *Twentieth Century Furniture Design* in 1988 was the publisher's initial foray into this subject area, followed by the Icon series and reference books such as *1000 Chairs* (1998), by Peter and Charlotte Fiell, now editors-in-charge of Taschen's

design titles. Taschen's commitment to con-temporary design extended to the interiors of flagship stores designed by Philippe Starck, which opened in Paris in September 2000 and Beverly Hills in November 2003. Others, particularly Phaidon, Thames & Hudson, and niche publishers such as 010 Publishers in Rotterdam, have also developed the market for design books, but through its non-elitist approach, it is Taschen that has popularized contemporary design most extensively. Thames & Hudson's *International Design Yearbook*, published annually since 1985, is a barometer of trends targeted at the design community more than general readers, chart-ing the trajectories of styles as well as design-ers' careers. A product of the 1980s design boom itself, for two decades the *Yearbook* has reinforced the star status of its guest editors, a status Andrée Putman detested even as she assumed the role in 1992. Ron Arad, Philippe Starck, Jasper Morrison, Ross Lovegrove, Karim Rashid and Marcel Wanders have been similarly fêted since 1990.

A star system operates amongst fashion as well as furniture designers, but the differ-ence is that fashion designers tend to be exclu-sively attached to one brand or fashion house, whereas the top furniture designers are gener-ally independent and work for a number of different companies. Where the two systems

Home Front, BBC, 2001. Photo: © BBC Photo Library.

VIP chair designed by Philip
Treacy, from the VIP (Very Important
Products) range, manufactured
by Habitat, UK, 2004. Foam
structure with wool upholstery.
Photo: courtesy of Habitat.

are similar is that the star designers' cache
increases the chances of success for the
companies that can afford to use them, and
they appear to operate a closed shop. The same
group of designers dominates all the catalogues of a small group of mostly Italian furniture manufacturers. Duncan Riches calls this
the 'Top 10 phenomenon' and recognizes it
as an aspect of brand building by the leading
manufacturers. 'All the Top 10, talented as they
are, are probably sometimes fallible, difficult,
lazy, incoherent, and unsure,' he writes.
'Maybe they aren't the "best" designers at all.
Perhaps they are just excellent all-rounders,
able to focus not just on the purities of form
and function, but on the nuts and bolts of
getting things made and finding a way to
tell people about them.'[14]

The media's celebration of design
accompanied a seismic shift in taste, especially
in Britain. Science, business and technology
journalist Virginia Postrel wrote about the
transformation she perceived in American
taste, where the combination of saturated markets, high income and sophisticated distribution techniques resulted in the increased aes-
theticization of everyday products and services
to differentiate them and increase their appeal
for niche-targeted customers. Contemporary
design became one tool amongst many in the
war for sales.[15] In Germany, Italy, Spain and
Scandinavia, modern design has always proved
popular in the mass market, but until the 1990s
the choice of contemporary furniture available
in British shops was extremely limited. Most
new furniture was bought from independent
retailers or department stores, not known for
their radical innovations. Flat-pack furniture
and out-of-town stores such as MFI and World
of Leather put affordable furniture within
reach of almost anyone. The effect of Terence
Conran's Habitat, founded in 1964, has been
well documented, but outside the metropolitan
centres it was less visible. Habitat lost its way
in the 1980s and in 1992 it was bought by the
Stichting Ingka Foundation, a Dutch-regis-
tered holding company that also owns IKEA.
In 1998 Tom Dixon became Habitat's Head
of Design and put Matthew Hilton, one of
Sheridan Coakley's original stable of designers
in the late 1980s, in charge of furniture. At
a stroke two of the leading-edge designers of
the previous 15 years entered the mainstream
of contemporary design. A plank of Dixon's
strategy was to reissue design classics from
the 1950s and 1960s, including furniture by
Robin Day and Pierre Paulin, appealing to the
1990s taste for retro-modern. He championed
the younger generation of designers too,
including the Azumis and Tord Boontje,
whose cut foil Garland lampshade launched
an international trend for ornate, foliate
decoration. For the 'Very Important Products'
collection, launched to celebrate the store's
40th anniversary in 2004, Dixon invited
celebrities and designers from other fields,
such as Stirling Moss, Manolo Blahnik, and
even his own boss Ingvar Kamprad, founder
of IKEA, to contribute furniture and product
designs. All these strategies served to make
Habitat more distinctive, appealing and fashionable on Britain's high streets, but it still
struggled to compete with the behemoth that
is IKEA, whose arrival in Britain on 1 October
1987 transformed home-furnishing taste.

That was the date the first British IKEA
store opened, in Warrington. It was followed
swiftly by a second at Brent Cross in north
London and by 2005 there were 13 stores

Crowds at the opening of the new
IKEA store, Edmonton, London,
Wednesday 9 February 2005.
Photo: Anne-Marie Sanderson.

IKEA advertisement, 'Elite Designers Against IKEA', 2004. Agency: Karmarama. Photo: Henrik Halvarsson / LundLund.

"Where is the soul in a £19 bedside table? Pah! It is nowhere."

I am Van den Puup, elite designer, and I know the difference between true and fraudulent design. True design like Van den Puup's is a friend of emotion, a foe of reason, laughs with wolves and cries with angels and is priced highly as any work of brilliance should be. Fraudulent design like IKEA's can be mildly attractive but lacks spirituality and is priced so low it can have no soul. I can see it all so clearly, but then I am a genius.

Van den Puup, Elite Designer

across the UK. *Blueprint* was quick to recognize the potential impact of the Swedish home store. 'IKEA is the company that has out-habitated Habitat around the world, and which, now that it has arrived in Britain, could finally challenge the anti-design preconceptions that dominate the bottom end of the British furniture market.'[16] And this IKEA did in abundance; by 2004 the company could claim UK sales had topped £1bn.[17] Economies of scale enable IKEA to keep prices very low, and although detractors derided the quality of some of its ranges, very many IKEA products were well-executed examples of contemporary design. In 1995, when it introduced its PS range of New Functionalist furniture and objects, IKEA was challenging the Italian high-end manufacturers on their own territory. Indeed Italian industrialists were already fearing the 'IKEA-effect' that high-design, low-cost furniture would have on their market.[18] IKEA could claim that one in ten Europeans were conceived in one of its beds, and it became difficult to find a British home *without* its furniture. Whether this was because of the prices, the perceived value for money, or an appreciation of affordable good design, it was clear the British public had a well-developed passion for Swedish furniture by the time IKEA opened in Edmonton in February 2005. A media campaign prior to the midnight grand opening of the store attracted some 7,000 shoppers, causing gridlock on surrounding roads and a riot as bargain hunters tried to enter the shop; five were hospitalized. 'I only came here to buy a cheap sofa', said one shopper. 'I was pushed to the ground and people clambered over me. I feared for my life.' Another shopper told the *Evening Standard*, 'I bought a sofa but when I turned my back someone stole it. I'm not upset. It's just furniture, not worth dying over.'[19] Cost seems to be the principal driver when consumers are drawn to buy contemporary furniture, especially if they sniff a bargain. Shoppers camped outside the London Vitra showroom for three days prior to its 2005 sale, hoping to snap up an Eames recliner and ottoman reduced from £4,000 to just £50. Much as at Edmonton, tempers flared when the doors opened, and blood was even shed as fights broke out over cut-price design classics. One shopper spotted someone trying to buy the £5 Tesco camping stools he had used in the queue but had abandoned in the crush. 'People have no idea what they're buying', he said. 'They think "It's in Vitra, it must be good. Buy it!"' Perhaps our taste is not as refined as our money-saving instinct.[20]

Each and every IKEA store is laid out in the same manner, making them cheaper to operate but eliminating local differences. One commentator observed that 'IKEA is locked in a spiral of success that shows little sign of reversing – the bigger it gets, the more the alternatives disappear.'[21] Rival low-cost retailers were overwhelmed; 154-year-old Courts was forced into receivership in 2004. In a series of high profile, eye-catching advertising campaigns IKEA waged war on traditional British taste, urging us to 'Chuck out your Chintz', and on elite designers (and their high prices). The latter campaign featured a fictional designer called Van den Puup, a caricature of Marcel Wanders' nationality, Karim Rashid's flamboyant dress sense but mostly Philippe Starck's physiognomy. IKEA not only changed what furniture was bought, but how it was bought. Like fashionable clothes, we can buy IKEA furniture, take it home, assemble it and use it on the same day, without waiting months for a piece to be made and delivered. The speed at which furniture is consumed has sped up since the 1960s, when people generally expected the bedroom, living room and dining suites they bought for their first home would last a lifetime. Today, the media and fashion system's obsession with novelty encourages us to expect shorter lifespans from our furniture, and to change our interiors much more frequently than in the past. Stores such as IKEA, that are able to offer low-priced goods that require less financial or emotional investment to buy them, can thrive in such a culture. IKEA, like its fashion counterparts on the High Street, Zara, H&M and Top Shop, defeat competition and woo customers through their size, economy of scale, speed of delivery and above all else, cost.

IKEA's success is global. In the rapidly developing Russian economy IKEA dominates the middle market, while those who wish to display their wealth choose high-end Italian brands such as Meritalia, which opened a store in St Petersburg in 2004. IKEA's products are the same here, but the company signed an agreement with the Ministry of Industry, Science and Technologies, undertaking to support the emerging Russian furniture manufacturing industry: it owns factories near St Petersburg and Moscow.[22]

With 70 stores, DFS claims to be Britain's biggest upholstery retailer and has employed contemporary design, together with persuasive credit terms, as a means of maintaining its market share. In 1998 a revealing article in its magazine *Sofastyle* sought to explain the semiotics of design to a general audience, by identifying four taste communities. 'A liking for big squashy sofas and chunky furniture, dark woods and warm colours identifies you as Middle Englander. Dependable, easy-going, nature-loving and sociable – this type are in the majority', it declared. In contrast 'a preference for more formal antique styles puts you in the Traditionalists bracket', but 'a taste for pale woods and light colours places you as a Modernist... You love to party and are not keen on squashy sofas because you just never have the time to lounge around. Yellow is a favourite colour.' Lastly 'minimalists can't stand clutter of any sort. The more avant garde type, they like to live in open plan rooms with lots of chrome and glass and leather. They are into black, white and grey plus some occasional splashes of strong, cool colour.' Somewhat simplistically, the retailer was nevertheless catering for conservative as well as more fashion-conscious customers and trying to educate them about their taste choices.[23] By 2005 DFS had teamed with TV interior-designer Linda Barker who was endorsing a modern and sleek collection, with far fewer traditional choices. Tellingly, the DFS magazine was now called *Designers Choice* and made much of the personalities of Barker and her associates. In television advertisements Barker underlined the rapid democratization of contemporary design: 'Design is there for everybody these days, it's not just the well informed,' she declared, because 'Our homes are everything and people want them to look *so* beautiful.'[24]

Large out-of-town retail parks are credited with the decline of traditional town centres and giants such as IKEA, or DFS, have met political resistance to opening new stores. In response, IKEA announced in 2005 that it would open new, smaller, stores near transport hubs or in town centres, heralding a new era for the company.[25] But Marks and Spencer embarked on the opposite strategy in February 2004, promising that its out-of-town Lifestores would be a new concept in lifestyle retailing. Given the increased design awareness of the British public, and an evident taste for contemporary style in the home, the time seemed right for a bold new furniture and furnishing store by the nation's favourite retailer. Why, then, did Lifestore fail?

A dream-team of powerful figures in British design was behind the project, led by Vittorio Radice, formerly CEO of Selfridges. The first vast new store, in Gateshead, was designed by John Pawson, and included a full-scale minimalist show-house as its centrepiece. *Wallpaper** founder Tyler Brûle handled

Display in Purves & Purves,
London, August 2005.
Photo: courtesy of Purves
& Purves.

communications and *Elle Decoration*'s Ilse Crawford was Creative Director in charge of styling the displays. Lifestore was organized around 'the rituals of everyday life rather than retail conventions'.[26] In actuality it featured zones based on concepts such as Renew, Celebrate and Alfresco, which in themselves were not difficult to understand, but seemed esoteric when compared to the Bathroom or Garden departments of more conventional stores. The product ranges were a rich mix of Italian, Swedish and Dutch design ideas, including own-brand furniture alongside products by the likes of Kartell and Magis. All the ingredients for success appeared to be present, but possibly the team overestimated the market for cutting-edge interiors in 'middle England'. Further stores were promised at Thurrock and Kingston upon Thames, but only six months after the Gateshead Lifestore opened, Marks and Spencer announced its impending closure and the cancellation of further plans. Sales had apparently reached only 30 per cent of expectations. Writing in the *Guardian* Caroline Roux commented that 'Good design is appropriate design and a little market research would probably have revealed that the people of Gateshead won't be reduced to a purse-opening swoon by a heavy dose of minimalism and a product range that includes a large amount of lacquer.'[27] IKEA appealed to the budget-conscious as well as the design-aware shopper and virtually single-handedly developed the mass market for contemporary furniture design in Britain. Perhaps Lifestore was too conceptual for the British public, who perceived it as luxury rather than necessity, and did not shop there. Marks and Spencer's recent history of financial instability, coupled with a shaky sense of identity, undoubtedly contributed to a loss of confidence in the boardroom that killed off Lifestore. In 2005 Marks and Spencer sold the 6,500 sq.m (70,000 sq.ft) Gateshead Lifestore, and a second at West Thurrock, to Danish furniture retailer Ilva, which aims to open 20 British furniture superstores over 10 years to rival IKEA.

At the top end of the market contemporary furniture had flourished through niche retailers such as Conran, Purves & Purves and Aram in London, De Padova in Milan and Vinçon in Barcelona. Notably each of these shops reflected the personal vision of its founder (as, indeed, IKEA reflected the vision of Ingvar Kamprad). These retailers acted as editors of product ranges, producing some of their own lines and buying-in others. More recently Murray Moss in New York has

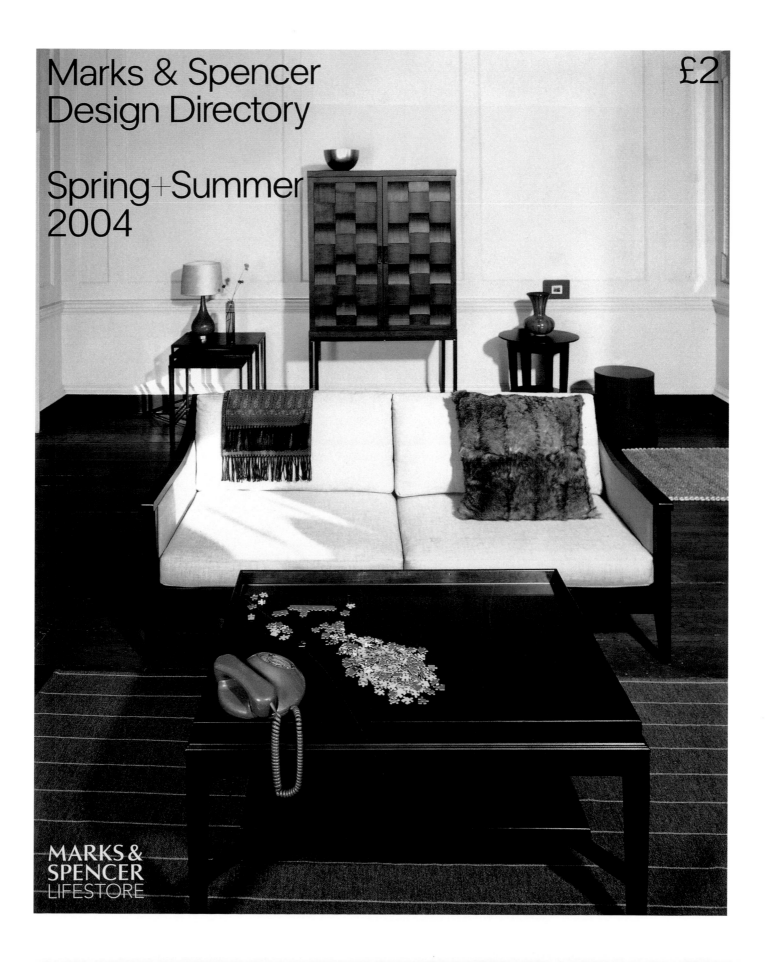

Marks & Spencer Design Directory, Spring/Summer 2004.

Exhibition for the launch of the Saturn Light designed by JAM at Same, Brick Lane, about 1998. Photo: courtesy of JAM.

Ron Arad retrospective exhibition at Barry Friedman Ltd, New York, 5 May–24 June 2005, including Big Heavy, 1989 and Eight by One, 1991. Photo: Spencer Tsai.

successfully combined a museum-like shop with the approach of an art-gallerist to promote design objects. He admits the influence of fashion retailing and the 'boutiquing of things', by which he means the grouping of merchandise not by function or type, but by mood and association, which was something that Lifestore tried too. In boutique environments Moss believes purchases are made not because customers need the items, but because they are buying into the lifestyle that the shop is promoting, whether it is fashionable clothes or high-end home furnishings, like his store.

Moss has succeeded where others did not: both Haus and Same in London, for example, were forward-looking furniture design shops launched in the mid-1990s era of 'Cool Britannia' but closed by 2000. The greatest challenge to design emporia has been the rise of virtual shopping on websites where overheads are low and high-value items such as furniture can be offered at lower prices than in shops in premium locations.[29] But internet shopping does not allow the consumer to test or fully experience the product, and is ill-suited as a medium for the sale of furniture. At best it offers the major retailers an alternative catalogue or virtual showroom. After the closure of Haus, which became the showroom for Ligne Roset, Jonathan Sherwood launched completelymodern.com, a web-based retailer of design-led products, with less focus on furniture and more emphasis on smaller, higher turnover product types. Piers Roberts and Rory Dodd had been the first in Britain to stock Droog Design and Snowcrash products in their Brick Lane shop, Same, opened in 1998. The Designers Block exhibition began as a promotional event for the shop, but greatly outlasted Same, which closed in 2000. Max Fraser's *Design UK* guides to design retailers (2001/2003) listed some 120 retailers across Britain, showing that the market, though not large, did exist beyond the metropolitan centres.

A network of design galleries also arose to nurture the very top end of the market, the area where furniture and design met and often merged with art. Gallery Mourmans in Maastricht, the Netherlands, directed by Ernest Mourmans, represents the one-off studio works and small batch productions of Ron Arad, Gaetano Pesce (who also designed the gallery itself in 1992), Ettore Sottsass and others. In 1985 Pierre Staudenmeyer founded the highly influential design gallery Neotu in Paris with another showroom in New York. Neotu produced editions of furniture by leading designers including Kristian Gavoille, Elizabeth Garouste and Mattia Bonetti, Eric Jourdan and Jasper Morrison for the upper reaches of the market. Gallery Kreo, founded in Paris by Clemente and Didier Krzentowski in 1992, followed a similar model with collections by James Irvine, the Bouroullec brothers, Michael Young and many more. Rendel and Spitz in Cologne was not a gallery per se, but was an advertising agency for design companies. Every year, to coincide with the Cologne Furniture Fair, an exhibition was held in the company's office which blended design manifestos and public relations, such as 'Blossoming Gap', a collaboration between Andrea Branzi and the Bouroullecs, staged in 2003. Gallery Klaus Engelhorn in Vienna represented both artists and designers. Its 2004 exhibition, 'Vanishing Point', teamed Jurgen Bey, Konstantin Grcic and the Viennese designer Robert Stadler (a collaborator in the Droog Design 'Do' project). Vanishing Point was a group of conceptual furniture and objects shown in Milan during the Salone del Mobile and later in Vienna. In London, gallerist David Gill represents designers and makers including Mattia Bonetti, one-time collaborator with Elizabeth Garouste.

These galleries represent a shifting trend away from antiques and towards twentieth-century and contemporary design. Traditionally, wealth and status were expressed by the accumulation of antiques and old masters. But today the new wealthy want to express different values, and prefer to match their collections of modern art and photography with contemporary furniture, or so believes Alexander Payne, head of 20–21st Century Design Art at the international auction house Phillips de Pury & Company.[30] Statistics bear him out: the Antique Collectors' Club, which monitors the trade in Britain, records falls in prices of 3 per cent in 2002 and a further 2 per cent in 2003.[31] Only the very top end of the trade thrives: prices for average 'brown furniture' have tumbled as more people choose modern and contemporary interior decoration over classic styles. Wealthy customers, Payne says, are looking for distinguished, innovative design works that will retain their value and mix well with the collections of other media. Payne describes this level of design as 'couture', borrowing directly from the language of fashion. The furniture is instantly recognizable, beautifully made, yet rare and therefore collectable. A major incentive to collectors is that contemporary furniture is still a fraction of the price of contemporary art,

'Vanishing Point 1', exhibition staged by Klaus Engelhorn 22 during the Milan Furniture Fair, 14-19 April 2004. Photo: Michael Turkiewicz.

but this is unlikely to remain the case. Art Deco furniture, for example, has many of the 'couture' characteristics Payne values, and is now amongst the most expensive furniture on the market. The small batches and unique, signed objects of today could top the market of tomorrow. Ron Arad designs furniture for mass-production but has always produced editions and one-offs for the collector's market, often of the same design but rendered in different materials. For art collectors his work can almost be regarded as sculpture rather than functional furniture, and in this respect he blazes a trail where other furniture designers are sure to follow. The conceptual works of designers from the Netherlands and elsewhere, for example, are also easily interpreted and assimilated by the art market. In 2005

Arad exhibited in New York for the first time since 1987, in a collaborative exhibition held at Phillips' fashionable Meat Packing District auction rooms and the Upper Eastside showroom of influential twentieth-century design dealer Barry Friedman. The event was another indicator of the rising stock of contemporary furniture design.[32]

Dennis Freedman, Creative Director of *W*, a fashion magazine published in New York, collects contemporary furniture and photography that fills his weekend house in the Hamptons. In a sense Freedman embodies the theme of this chapter: he brings the attitudes of the fashion system to bear on his taste for furniture. He dislikes what he describes as 'timid' design, preferring instead furniture that represents updated traditions and which has presence, such as the work of André Dubreuil and Tom Dixon. 'What I find incredibly boring', he said, 'is contemporary furniture that is minimal and Miesian and simply an exercise in refinement. If you want that, go back to Bauhaus where there really was a change in thinking and things were provocative in the true sense of the word. Today, having those elegantly refined pieces is kind of indicative of boring good taste… Usually money and studied, careful, good taste is a disastrous combination. It only means you will get something that is kind of faultless, really uninteresting.'[33] Freedman, on the other hand, prefers eclectic interiors with personality, and he is almost negligent with his own collection, for example the nine Campana Brothers pieces he bought but has never had delivered from São Paolo. Another recent addition was from the solo show Maarten Baas staged at Murray Moss in 2004. Freedman acquired a charred version of Charles Rennie Mackintosh's high-backed chair designed for the bedroom at Hill House in 1903. The authored, 'signature' design appeals to Freedman, and collectors like him. They are no longer fans of New Functionalism (if they ever were) but may be attracted by the 'new antiques', probably because the symbolic value of such furniture allies it to art, and to fashion.

What happens to all the furniture and 'things with attitude' we see in showrooms, magazines and catalogues once they are taken home? Undoubtedly contemporary design has become the signifier of new ways of living, like the relaxed-yet-experimental urban loft-living style that has been translated to new-build suburban housing estates, or the period homes that include home-offices and IT workstations to rival the most high-tech corporate headquarters. *The Furniture Machine* has shown how complex the contemporary furniture industry is today. Style trends are not autonomous but are complex cultural creations. The furniture that is bought flat-pack at IKEA shares traits with the rarest conceptual object found in a gallery. Both are subject to market forces, even if the markets, and the forces, are radically different. Both are the creations of designers, but designers do not and cannot operate alone. Both are subject to material and technical innovations that may make them cheaper, or more expensive, depending on the application. I cannot predict what furniture will dominate the next two decades, but it is likely it will begin at the margins of the industry, the preserve of an informed elite, before making its way into mainstream fashion. Furniture for the mass market and for the elite is all part of a vast network of designers, manufacturers, educators, media agencies, taste makers, trade fairs, gallerists, marketers and retailers that together shape the furniture we read about, that we aspire to, that we own and that ultimately we replace with something new.

Interior of Dennis Freedman's house. Photo: Marcelo Krasilcic.

Murray Moss

'Having an audience, whether in a theatre or in a store, is a privilege and a responsibility that should not be wasted. It is the retailer's job to guide them through a meaningful set of experiences!' [1]

Originally an actor in New York, in 1978 Moss founded a successful fashion label with the Dutch designer Ronaldus Shamask that eventually took him to Italy to work with producers. He sold the fashion trademark in 1990 but wanted to continue collaborating with Italian manufacturers. 'At this moment, certain fashion houses were suggesting a synergy between fashion design and interior design, with the first "home" collections,' he recalled. 'I understood that this indicated a direction, that the emergence of "lifestyle" fashion marketing suggested that various disciplines should converge at some point.' [2] His idea was to persuade famous New York fashion stores to expand their homeware lines under his guidance, but when none of them signed up, Moss opened his first eponymous store in Greene Street, SoHo, in 1994. In a sea of conservativism, Moss was a beacon of advanced European design and taste. The Moss store was deliberately positioned at the epicentre of the New York contemporary art world. At the time contemporary design, particularly design-led Italian brands like Flos (lighting) and Venini (glass), did not command much custom in the traditionalist American market. Moss hoped that by positioning the products as art he would help customers to see them with less prejudice. What is more, he styled his shop as a museum, with locked cases and uniformed attendants, adding prestige to the objects he sold; 'In short I was demanding more attention from the viewer'. Expansion in 1999 allowed Moss to display furniture, by Edra, Moroso and others. The larger store also allowed his celebrated, theatrical window displays to become fully fledged exhibitions. These are credited with

introducing cutting-edge European designers to an ever-more receptive American audience, including Maarten Baas in 2004 and Tord Boontje in 2005.

The Moss store is a distillation of its owner's taste and passions, ranging from large-scale furniture and lighting through to tableware, accessories, books and textiles. It is a Kunstkammer for today. Neither the shop, nor the separate gallery space opened nearby in 2005, is solely devoted to contemporary design. Many of the artefacts are historic designs that, for Moss, resonate with contemporary objects – for example, the ceramics made in the Nymphenburg factory in Germany.

'The End' exhibition of work by Tord Boontje, 9 February–20 March 2005, including Witch chair, Doll chair, Revolution swivel chair, Come Rain Come Shine chandelier and a unique table, all manufactured by Moroso, Italy. Photo: Davies + Starr.

ShimmerGlimmerTwinkleSparkleShine! exhibition of lighting from the Swarovski Crystal Palace collection, 9 January–12 March 2006. Photo: Davies + Starr.

As New York's leading tastemaker, Moss leads a movement away from low-cost high-design (epitomized by the ubiquity of 'designer' plastic chairs) towards romantic, decorative objects where function is almost immaterial. Increasingly he has found himself 'loosening up the pretence of function' that was the dogma of modern design during the twentieth century. He championed the pretty floral aesthetics of Tord Boontje and Hella Jongerius, for example, as well as Nymphenburg's figurines, which he rehabilitated from being regarded as kitsch. At the same time, he does not refute the accusation that his store is elite, as he does not claim to be promoting democratic design. 'We live in a world where most people can't afford to buy the cheapest thing at Target,' he reasons, while frankly admitting the designs he sells are luxuries.[3]

'The End' exhibition of work by Tord Boontje, 9 February–20 March 2005, including Copper Blossom chandelier, Happy Rocker chair, manufactured by Moroso, Italy. The Favela mural by Humberto and Fernando Campana is also visible. Photo: Davies + Starr.

General view of the interior of Moss, including Mummy chairs by Peter Traag, Carte Blanche table by Ann Demeulemeester, 606 Universal shelving by Vitsoe, Pluma Cubic lamp by Helke Buchfelder and Random Lights by Bertjan Pot. Photo: Davies + Starr.

Ilse Crawford

'There's no such thing as a typical consumer. Consumers are a lot more up for things that are "out there" than you would think.' [1]

Ilse Crawford is difficult to classify, but more than anything she is a design proselytizer. Through careers as a design journalist, creative director, teacher and designer she has been instrumental in bringing contemporary design into the mainstream.

Crawford ran an architect's practice and worked on the *Architect's Journal* and *World of Interiors* before she became the founding editor of *Elle Decoration* in 1989. Her innovation for the magazine was to photograph real homes and the people who lived there. These were lived-in interiors, quite unlike the sanitized and dehumanized photographs most architectural magazines published. The democratic approach aimed to appeal to the same trend-conscious market that bought the fashion magazine *Elle*, from which the publication grew. The time was right for a fresh approach to interior design, and Crawford recalled that this was a generation who were better educated, richer and better travelled than any before them, and more willing and able to experiment with their homes. [2]

Elle Decoration appeared at the same moment as a generation of younger British design talent, and Crawford was its champion. Ron Arad, Tom Dixon and John Pawson were favourites. [3] The *Elle Deco* philosophy was to mix old and new, expensive and affordable. Crawford aimed to empower her readers to create interiors that reflected their personalities. The same desire to inform and inspire lay behind the television make-over shows that followed *Elle Decoration* and appealed to the same market.

For two years after she left *Elle Decoration*, until 2000, Crawford lived in New York to form a homeware collection for Donna Karan. She found that, though Karan was enthusiastic to extend her brand beyond clothing, the fast-moving fashion system was unable to accommodate the longer lead times needed to develop products such as furniture. Back in Europe in 2000, after a brief period with *Bare* magazine, Crawford was appointed to head the 'Man and Well-being' course at the Design Academy Eindhoven. Here she could develop her holistic ideas about design that she first expressed in a book, *Sensual Home*, in 1997. Under the banner 'Form Follows Feeling' Crawford encouraged her students to find a design language based foremost on emotions. By now Crawford was designing her own interiors, most notably for the Soho House chain of private members clubs in London, New York and elsewhere. She found it impossible to find what she called 'glamorous and sexy modern

The Other cabinet, designed by studioilse, manufactured by Baleri Italia, Italy, 2005. MDF, steel feet, mirror, lacquered interior; 36-24-36 fabric, designed by studioilse, manufactured by Christopher Farr Cloth, UK, 2005. Linen. Photo: Hamish Fraser.

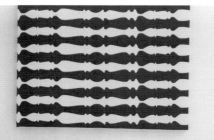

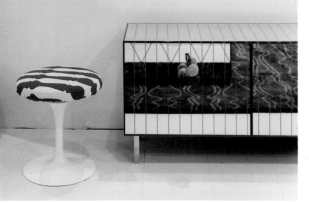

furniture' so began to design it herself, for
production under her own name and for
Baleri Italia.[4] Crawford's designs revealed
her admiration for contemporary Dutch
design such as Marcel Wanders' 'new antiques'
as well as for mid-century modern furniture.

Crawford wonders whether an increasing
number of women in key roles in the furniture
industry, both as consumers and as producers,
are instrumental in bringing it closer to the
sensibility of the fashion system. It is certainly
true that the presence of women such as
Crawford in the industry does much to dispel
the impression of furniture design as an annex
of architecture or engineering.

Bedroom in Soho House New
York, concept design by studioilse,
2003. Photo: Martyn Thompson.

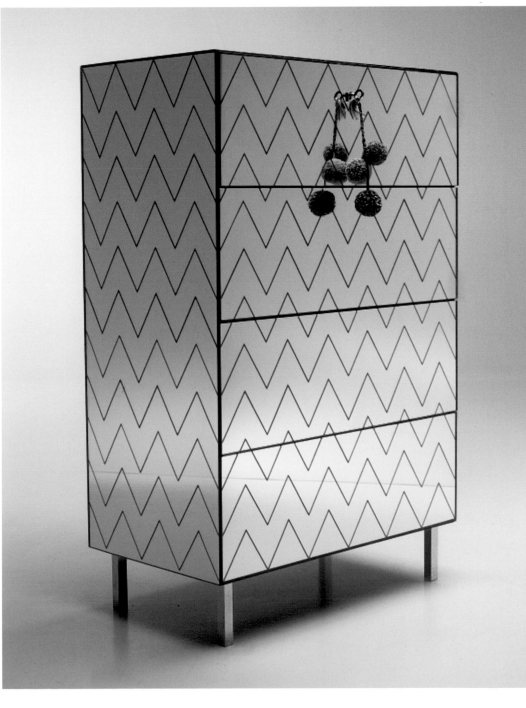

36-24-36 table, designed and
manufactured by studioilse,
UK, 2005. MDF, rubberwood,
polyurethane lacquer. Photo:
courtesy of studioilse.

The Other chest of drawers,
designed by studioilse,
manufactured by Baleri Italia,
Italy, 2005. MDF, steel feet,
mirror, lacquered interior.
Photo: courtesy of studioilse.

The Furniture Machine

Bibliography

Magazines and Periodicals

Abitare (Milan, 1960-)
Azimuts: research and design review
(Saint Etienne, 1991-)
Blueprint (London, 1983-)
Domus (Milan, 1929-)
Elle Decoration (London, 1989-)
Frame (Amsterdam, 1999)
Icon (London, 2003)
ID - International Design (New York, 1984)
The International Design Yearbook
    (New York, 1985-)
Interni (Milan, 1967-)
Intramuros (Paris, 1985-)
Metropolis (New York, 1981-)
Ottagono (Milan, 1986-)
Surface (San Francisco, 1996?-)
Wallpaper* (London, 1996-)

Books

Albus, V. and Fischer, V., *13 Nach
Memphis: design zwischen Askese und
Sinnlichkeit* (Munich, 1995)

Albus, V., *The Bookworm by Ron Arad*
(Frankfurt, 1997)

Annink, E. and Schwartz, I. (eds.), *Bright
Minds, Beautiful Ideas: Bruno Munari, Charles
& Ray Eames, Martí Guixé* (Amsterdam, 2003)

Antonelli, P., *Mutant Materials in
Contemporary Design* (New York, 1995)

Antonelli, P., *Objects of Design from The
Museum of Modern Art* (New York, 2003)

Antonelli, P., *Safe: design takes on risk*
(New York, 2005)

Arad, A. and Collings, M., *Ron Arad talks
to Matthew Collings* (London, 2004)

Asensio Cerver, F., *The New Modern
Furniture Design* (Barcelona, 1998)

Attfield, J., *Wild Things: the material
culture of everyday life* (Oxford, 2000)

Aveline, M.(ed.), *Elizabeth Garouste
et Mattia Bonetti* (Paris, 1990)

Bakker, G. and Ramakers, R. (eds.),*Droog
Design: spirit of the nineties* (Rotterdam, 1998)

Bakker, G. and Ramakers, R. (eds.), *Couleur
Locale: Droog Design for / für Oranienbaum*
(Amsterdam, 1999)

Barley, N. *et al* (eds), *Lost and Found: critical
voices in new British design* (London, 1999)

Barry Friedman Ltd and Phillips de Pury
& Company exhibition catalogue *Ron Arad*
(New York, 2005)

Ber Tacchini, G. et al., *The Official Point of
View: Milano furniture fair 2002* (Milan, 2002)

Betsky, A. and Eeuwens, A., *False Flat:

why Dutch design is so good (London, 2004)

Böhm, F. (ed.), *KGID Konstantin Grcic
Industrial Design* (London, 2005)

Boissiere, O., *Starck* (Köln, 1991)

Boissiere, O. and Guidot, R., *Ron Arad,*
(Paris, 1997)

Bongaerts, U. (ed.), *Goethe / Grcic:
quotidian objects* (Milan, 2000)

Bordignon, E. (ed.), *Luxury in Living:
Italian designers for Italian industries*
(Milan, 2005)

Bouroullec, E. and Bouroullec, R. *et al, Ronan
and Erwan Bouroullec* (London, 2003)

Boyer, C. A. and Zanco, F., *Jasper Morrison*
(Paris, 1999)

Boym, C., *Curious Boym: design works*
(New York, 2002)

Branzi, A., *Domestic Animals: the neo-
primitive style* (Cambridge, Mass., 1987)

Branzi, A., *Learning from Milan: design and the
second modernity* (Cambridge, Mass., 1988)

Byars, M., *50 chairs: innovations in design
and materials* (Hove, 1997)

Cassagnau, P., and Pillet, C. (eds), *Starck's

Kids (Paris, 1999)

Collins, M., *Tom Dixon* (London, 1990)

Conran, T., and Fraser, M., *Designers on Design* (London, 2004)

Crafts Council exhibition catalogue *Flexible Furniture* (London, 1997)

Crafts Council exhibition catalogue *No Picnic* (London, 1998)

Crafts Council exhibition catalogue *Furniture, Jerwood Applied Arts Prize 1999* (London, 1999)

Crafts Council exhibition catalogue *Home Sweet Home: contemporary British design for the home* (London, 2001)

Crafts Council exhibition catalogue *Furniture, Jerwood Applied Arts Prize 2004* (London, 2004)

Craig Miller, R. (ed.), *US Design 1975-2000* (Munich, 2002)

Cranz, G., *The Chair: rethinking culture, body, and design* (New York, 1998)

Crasset, M., *Matali Crasset un pas de côté 91/02* (Lausanne, 2002)

Crasset, M., *Design & Designer: Matali Crasset* (Paris, 2003)

Dixon, T., *Rethink* (London, 2000)

Dormer, P., *Furniture Today: its design and craft* (London, 1995)

Doveil, F. (ed.), *iMade: material innovation in the Italian furniture industry* (Milan, 2000 / 2001)

Downey, C. A., *Neo furniture* (London, 1992)

Dunne, A., *Hertzian Tales: electronic products, aesthetic experience and critical design* (London, 1999)

Dunne, A., and Raby, F., *Design Noir: the secret life of electronic objects* (London, 2001)

Duits, Thimo Te. (ed.), *The Origin of Things: sketches, models, prototypes* (Rotterdam, 2003)

Eidelberg, M. (ed.), *Design for Living: furniture and lighting 1950-2000* (Paris, 2000)

Fiell, C. and P., *1000 Chairs*, (Köln, 1997)

Fiell, C. and P. (eds.), *Designing the 21st century* (Köln, 2001)

Gramigna, G., *Repertorio del Design Italiano 1950-2000 per l'Arredamento Domestico* (Turin, 2003)

Greenhalgh, P. (ed.), *The Persistence of Craft* (London, 2002)

Guillaume, V. (ed.), *Starck in Words* (Paris, 2003)

Habegger, J., and Osman, JH., *Sourcebook of Modern Furniture* (third edition, New York, 2005)

Hagströmer, D., *Swedish Design* (Stockholm, 2001)

Hall, G., and Snowman, MR. (eds.), *Avant Premiere: contemporary French furniture* (London, 1988)

Hans, I. and Hinte, E. van, *Black Bazaar: design dilemmas* (Rotterdam, 2003)

Hershberg, S. (ed.), *My World, the new subjectivity in design* (London, 2005)

Hinte, E. van (ed.), *Eternally Yours: visions on product endurance*, (Rotterdam, 1997)

Hinte, E. van (ed.), *Richard Hutten* (Rotterdam, 2002)

Hinte, E. van (ed.), *Eternally Yours: time in design, product value sustenance* (Rotterdam, 2004)

Hinte, E. van, *ARCO 12. Dutch Designers do Furniture* (Rotterdam, 2005)

Hinte, E. van, Rijk, T. de, Jager, I., *Under Cover, evolution of upholstered furniture* (Rotterdam, 2006)

Joris, YGJM. (ed.), *Sense of Wonder: chi ha paura...?* ('s-Hertogenbosch, 2002)

Joris, YGJM. (ed.), *Wanders Wonders* ('s-Hertogenbosch, 1999)

Jousset, M., *La Donation Kartell* (Paris, 2000)

Jousset, M. (ed.), *La Collection de Design du Centre Georges Pompidou* (Paris, 2001)

Lazzaroni, L., *35 Years of Design at Salone del Mobile* (Milan, 1996)

McDermott, C., *Matthew Hilton: furniture for our time* (London, 2000)

Meneguzzo, M. (ed.), *Philippe Starck Distordre: conversation about design between Alberto Alessi and Philippe Starck* (Crusinallo, Italy, 1996)

Morgan, CL., *Starck* (New York, 1999)

Morgan, CL., *Marc Newson* (London, 2003)

Morrison, J., *Everything but the walls: Jasper Morrison* (Baden, 2002)

Müller Stahl, J. (ed.), *Dish: international design for the home* (New York, 2005)

Novembre, F., *Fabio Novembre* (Amsterdam, 2001)

Pavitt, J., *Brilliant: lights and lighting* (London, 2004)

Payne, A. (ed.), *Azumi: ideas=book* (London, 1999)

Postrel, V., *The Substance of Style* (New York, 2003)

Ramakers, R. (ed.), *Simply Droog: 10 + 1 years of creating, innovation and discussion* (Amsterdam, 2004)

Rashid, K., *I want to change the world* (New York and London, 2001)

Rawsthorn, A., *Marc Newson* (London, 1999)

Redhead, D., *Products of Our Time* (London, 1999)

Redhead, D., *Industry of One: designer-makers in Britain 1981-2001* (London, 2001)

Röhsska Museet exhibition catalogue *Björn Dahlström* (Göteburg, 2001)

Severen, M. Van. (ed.), *Maarten Van Severen* (Ghent and Amsterdam, 2000)

Skov Holt, S., and Holt Skov, M., *Blobjects and Beyond: the new fluidity in design* (San Francisco, 2005)

Sudjic, D., *Ron Arad: restless furniture* (London, 1989)

Sudjic, Deyan, *Ron Arad*, (London, 1999)

Thackara, J. (ed.), *Design After Modernism: beyond the object* (London, 1988)

Vanlaethem, F., *Gaetano Pesce: architecture, design, art* (London, 1989)

Vlassenrood, L. (ed.), *Reality Machines: mirroring the real in contemporary Dutch architecture, photography and design* (Rotterdam, 2003)

Walrecht, B., *Home Made Holland* (London, 2002)

Zuber-Cupissol, M., *Plaidoyer pour le mobilier contemporain: L'Atelier de Recherche et de Création du Mobilier National 1964-2000* (Paris, 2001)

Notes

Introduction

1   *The International Design Yearbook*, 1998, p.75
2   Judy Attfield, *Wild Things: The Material Culture of Everyday Life*, 2000
3   'Italy: the New Domestic Landscape; achievements and problems of Italian design', MoMA, New York, 26 May–11 September 1972, catalogue by Emilio Ambasz
4   Editorial, *Blueprint*, 50, September 1988, p.7
5   See James Woodhuysen and Jane Lamacraft, 'Shuffling Armchairs on the *Titanic*', special report about challenges facing the British furniture industry, *Blueprint*, 57, May 1989, pp.42–6
6   *Blueprint*, 62, November 1989, p.40
7   *The International Design Yearbook*, 1989–90, p.44
8   A major exhibition of the Eameses' work was staged at the Design Museum, London, 15 September 1998–4 January 1999. *Blueprint*, 153, September 1998, included a major feature on the Eames House by Beatriz Colomina, excerpted from a new book by her, and articles about where to buy Vitra re-editions and vintage pieces through auctions and dealers.
9   Attfield, op. cit., p.30
10 Alice Rawsthorn, *Marc Newson*, 1999, p.12
11 Profile by Alex Wiltshire, *Icon*, 31, January 2006, pp.48–52
12 The new trend in Swedish design was explored in 'Beauty and the Beast: New Swedish Design', The Crafts Council, London, 18 November 2004–6 February 2005.
13 'Import Export, Global Influences in Contemporary Design', British Council tour and Victoria and Albert Museum, London, 20 September–4 December 2005
14 Source: Population Division of the Department of Economic and Social Affairs of the United Nations Secretariat, *World Population Prospects: The 2004 Revision and World Urbanization Prospects: The 2003 Revision*;http://esa.un.org/unpp/p2kOdata.asp
15 Dinah Casson, 'The annual search for the impossible at IDI', *Blueprint*, 68, June 1990, p.10
16 Source: www.worldfurniture online.com/dbsys/services/fairs.html. The calendar covers exhibitions of contract furniture, office furniture, home furniture, kitchens and bathroom furniture, upholstered furniture, furnishings, light fixtures and wood-working machinery.
17 Figures taken from *Luxury in Living: Italian Designers for Italian Industries*, 2005, appendix about trade bodies, no page number
18 Tito Armellini, secretary of Ifi, quoted by Manlio Armellini, 'The Meaning of a Story', in Laura Lazzaroni, *35 Years of Design at Salone del Mobile*, 1996, no page number.
19 Lazzaroni, ibid., p.19
20 2004 figures: Cologne, 1369 exhibitors and 120,000 visitors (Source, Koelnmesse GmbH); Milan, 1973 exhibitors and 189,655 visitors (Source, Cosmit SpA)
21 Email to author, 22 March 2005
22 100% Design, London, 2005, 35,209 visitors; Stockholm Furniture Fair, 2005, 36,447 visitors; Salon du Meuble, Paris, 2003, 40,500 visitors; ICFF, New York, 2003, 17,000 visitors; Kortrijk Interieur Biennale, 2002, 110,051 visitors (sources: fair organizers / *Icon*, 9, January 2004)
23 From an interview by Fiona Sibley, February 2004, www.hiddenart.com/news/interviews/designersblock
24 Marcus Fairs and Kieran Long, 'Milan Top 10', *Icon*, 24, June 2005, p.51
25 Interview with the author, 4 October 2005

1 Appropriation

1   Ettore Sottsass, 'Leaving the Grotto', forward to *Ron Arad Associates: One Off Three*, 1993
2   Nigel Coates, 'Street Signs' in John Thackara (ed.), *Design After Modernity*, 1988, p.109
3   Ron Arad quoted by Nonie Niesewand in *The International Design Yearbook*, 1989–90, p.18
4   For a fuller genealogy of appropriation in art, architecture and design see Michael Collins, 'In Praise of Danger'

in *Tom Dixon*, 1990, pp.76-87
5   From Lesley Thomson, 'Weld of Interiors', *Time Out*, 4-11 May 1988, p.119; cited in Collins, op. cit., p.84
6   Collins, op. cit., p.77
7   Nigel Coates, from the first issue of *Albion* magazine published by NATØ, 1983; cited in Collins, op cit., p.78. See also Nigel Coates, 'Street Signs' in John Thackara (ed.), *Design After Modernity*, 1988, pp.95-114, for an evocation of the period.
8   *The International Design Yearbook*, 1996, p.19
9   *Blueprint*, 115, March 1995, p.18
10 Tom Dixon, *Rethink*, 2000, p.19
11 Marco Romanelli, *Domus*, 766, December 1994, p.55
12 *Domus*, 767, January 1995, p.53; *The International Design Yearbook*, 1993, p.19
13 Jasper Morrison, *Everything but the Walls*, 2002, p.11
14 Nick Barley *et al*. *Lost and Found: critical voices in new British Design*, pp.72-3
15 'Mies Meets Marx: mmm An Installation by Michael Marriott', Geffrye Museum, London, 26 September 2002-19 January 2003
16 Tim Parsons, 'Good Company', www.mrparsons.co.uk, 2001; David Redhead, *Industry of One: Designer-Makers in Britain* 1981-2001, Crafts Council, 2001
17 *No Picnic*, Crafts Council, 1998, section 02; Gareth Williams, 'Creating Lasting Values' in Paul Greenhalgh (ed.), *The Persistence of Craft*, 2002, pp.68-70
18 Quoted in Nick Barley *et al*., op. cit., p.70
19 Constantin and Laurene Leon Boym were inspired by the heaps of discarded packing materials on the street around their studio in New York's Meat Packing District to use the same polypropylene strapping as Boontje to make a chair (Strap Chair, 1996). Boontje was exploiting its symbolic value as much as its materiality, but the Boyms were more concerned with it as an experimental material. See Constantin Boym, *Curious Boym*, 2002, pp.42-51. Ali Tayar also found inspiration in the detritus of the Meat Packing District. Nea Table 1 was made of particleboard pallet he found on the street. See Paolo Antonelli, *Mutant Materials in Contemporary Design*, 1995, p.101; Phillips, New York, 19 November 2002, lot 5.

20 'You can't lay down your memories' was made in an edition of 16, issued by by Droog Design. No.16 of the edition was auctioned at Phillips, New York, 19 November 2002, lot 6. Renny Ramakers, *Droog Design, Spirit of the Nineties*, 1998, pp.38, 54-5; Gareth Williams, 'Use it Again', in Renny Ramakers (ed.), *Simply Droog, 10+1 years of creating innovation and discussion*, 2004, pp.23-34; Paola Antonelli, *Objects of Design from the Museum of Modern Art*, 2003, p.276
21 Volker Albus and Volker Fischer, *13 Nach Memphis*, 1995, p.58
22 In 2005 N2 reported that the Pof 1 chair would be put into production by Horgen Glarus. E-mail correspondence with the author and Jörg Boner of N2, 17 August 2005.
23 Philippe Starck quoted in Nonie Niesewand, *The International Design Yearbook*, 1990-91, p.89
24 Marcus Fairs, profile of Maarten Baas, *Icon*, 20, February 2005, pp.54-60
25 Baas showed some more Smoke furniture in the studio of Fabio Novembre during the 2005 Milan Furniture Fair and a further collection with Murray Moss at the Art Basel Miami Beach fair, 1-4 December 2005.

Jurgen Bey

1   Jurgen Bey interviewed by Ineke Schwartz, in Ed Annink and Ineke Schwartz (eds.), *Bright Minds, Beautiful Ideas*, 2003, p.18
2   Ineke Schwartz, 'Cracking the codes of reality: an interview with Jurgen Bey', ibid, p.178

Marcel Wanders

1   Droog Design catalogue 2000, p.16
2   Marcel Wanders, *Wanders Wonders*, 1999, p.15

2   New Functionalism

1   Charles Arthur Boyer and Federica Zanco, *Jasper Morrison*, 1999, pp.48-9
2   David Redhead, 'The irresistible rise of the anonymous', *Blueprint*, 100, September 1993, p.79
3   Nonie Niesewand, *The International Design Yearbook*, 1989-90, p.11
4   Editorial, 'When the music stops', *Blueprint*, 50, September 1988, p.7
5   *Ron Arad talks to Matthew Collings*, 2004, p.11
6   John Pawson, 'Judd and the Art of Reason', *Blueprint*, 99, July-August 1993, pp.32-4
7   Geert Bekaert, 'Hors d'âge. The Work of Maarten Van Severen', in *Maarten Van Severen*, 2000, p.69
8   Caroline Roux, 'Solitary Refinement', *Blueprint*, 115, March 1995, pp.32-5
9   Aiden Walker, 'On form in Flanders', *Blueprint*, 181, March 2001, pp.30-2
10 Boyer and Zanco, ibid., p.41
11 Jasper Morrison, *Everything but the walls*, 2002, p.7
12 Lucy Bullivant, 'Grcic Logic', *Designer's Journal*, April 1992, pp.42-4
13 David Redhead, 'The Mouse That Roars', *Blueprint*, 121, October 1995, p.36
14 David Redhead, 'The art of Human Geometry', *Blueprint*, 111, October 1994, p.45
15 'Milan's strange sense of déjà vu', *Blueprint*, 41, October 1987, p.10
16 David Redhead, 'Foreign Exchange', *Blueprint*, 96, April 1993, pp.34-6
17 'Domus Forum: concerning production design', *Domus*, 759, April 1994, pp.119-22. A panel of leading industrialists including Giulio Cappellini, Enrico Baleri, Carlo Guglielmi, Enrico Astori and Rodrigo Rodriguez convened to discuss the challenges that lay before the Italian furniture industry.
18 Rick Poyner, 'The well ordered world of Antonio Citterio', *Blueprint*, 48, June 1988, pp.38-42
19 David Redhead, 'Foreign Exchange', *Blueprint*, 96, April 1993, pp.34-6
20 CBI catalogue, 1997
21 Interview with the author, 16 February 2005; profile by Alex Wiltshire, *Icon*, 18, December 2004, pp.96-102
22 Author interview, op. cit.
23 Barber Osgerby also competed against (and beat) Azumi for the 'Furniture Designer of the Year' award at the 2005 Blueprint Sessions, organized by *Blueprint* magazine in March 2005. The third nominee was Patricia Urquiola.
24 Michelle Ogundehin, 'Lightness and Shade', *Blueprint*, 127, April 1996, p.17
25 Letter to the author from Tomoko Azumi, 7 July 1997, Department of Furniture, Textiles and Fashion Information Section, V&A

Jasper Morrison

1 Jasper Morrison, interview with Brigitte Fitoussi, June 1995: *L'architecture d'Aujourd'hui*, No.300, September 1995, cited in Charles Arthur Boyer and Federica Zanco, *Jasper Morrison*, Paris, 1999, p.29
2 Boyer and Zanco, ibid, p.73
3 Peter Dormer, *Jasper Morrison - Designs, Projects and Drawings 1981-1989*, 1990; cited in Boyer and Zanco, p.73
4 Ibid.

Konstantin Grcic

1 'Three generations at the Vitra Design Museum', *Intramuros*, April-May 1997, pp.20-3
2 Ibid.
3 *Elle Decoration*, October 1998, p.43
4 For a full examination of the design process for Chair One see Florian Böhm (ed.), *KGID Konstantin Grcic Industrial Design*, 2005, pp.198-215
5 Interview with Konstantin Grcic by Constance Rubini, *Azimuts, Research and Design Review*, 25, June 2005, pp.73-6; 'sit-on sculpture', *Frame*, 44, May-June 2005

3   Neo-Pop

1 Marc Newson in Alice Rawsthorn, *Marc Newson*, 1999, p.9, Marc Newson in Simon Mills, 'Watch this space', *Sunday Times Magazine*, 27 November 1994, pp.60-5
2 Karim Rashid, *The International Design Yearbook*, 2003, p.14
3 The production histories of design classics can be complex. The Pantower was made by Vitra in Europe and Herman Miller in the US during 1969 and 1970 only. From 1970 to 1975 Fritz Hansen made it in Denmark. In 1997 it was manufactured briefly by Stega in Switzerland, before the Vitra Design Museum (subtly separate from Vitra itself) assumed production from 1999 to the present day. The last period of manufacture, therefore, has been the most sustained for this design. Source: author correspondence with Vitra UK, 10 March 2005
4 *The International Design Yearbook*, 1999, p.70

5 www.designmuseum.org/design/index
6 Alice Rawsthorn, op. cit., p.12
7 *Jasper Morrison, Marc Newson, Michael Young*, Reykavik Art Museum, 1999. The one-off white-painted set of Young's MY 068 chairs, made for this exhibition, were included for auction by Phillips, New York, 19 November 2002, lot 3
8 Giulio Cappellini in *Ronan and Erwan Bouroullec*, 2003, p.13
9 For more on the relationship between neo-Pop and 1960s Pop design, with particular reference to inflatables, see Gareth Williams, 'Software' in *Swell*, 1998, pp.19-21
10 Ross Lovegrove, Moooi catalogue, 2005
11 The furniture and fittings of the Skoda boutique were auctioned by Phillips, New York, 19 November 2002, lot 8.
12 Advertising copy for the Safari seating read 'An imperial piece inside your squalid home walls. A more beautiful piece than you. A beautiful piece you don't really deserve. Clear your sitting room! And clear your lives too!' Quoted by Laura Lazzorini, *35 Years of Design at Salone del Mobile*, 1996, p.33
13 Rowan Moore, 'The psychoanalysis of an Alessi kettle', *Blueprint*, 99, July-August 1993, p.12
14 Phil Patton in Steven Skov Holt and Mara Holt Skov, *Blobjects and Beyond: the New Fluidity in Design*, San Francisco, 2005, pp.157-67
15 Christopher Mount, 'French Kissing in the USA' in *Starck in Words*, 2003, p.109
16 Alex Wilshire, profile of Jerszy Seymour, *Icon*, 22, April 2005, pp.100-8
17 Steven Skov Holt and Mara Holt Skov, op. cit., p.57
18 Steven Skov Holt, ibid., p.147
19 See Paola Antonelli, *Objects of Design from the Museum of Modern Art*, 2003, pp.132 and 135
20 *Ron Arad talks to Matthew Collings*, 2004, pp.23-4
21 Peter Popham, 'Ron Arad's Restless Furniture', review of the 'Breeding in Captivity' exhibition at the Edward Totah Gallery, London, *Blueprint*, 96, April 1993, p.39
22 Ron Arad Studio price list, 1995
23 Matthew Collings, '... in the field of design it's really you: wonky curved lines; a flamboyant curve - an exaggerated sign of… what is it? Being an "individual". It seems to be a deliberate attention-grabbing opposite to Minimalism.' *Ron Arad talks to Matthew*

Collings, 2004, p.228
24 Mirko Zardini, 'Zaha Hadid in 5x2, 5x0,75 metri', off print from *Interni*, 500, April 2000
25 Jennifer Kabat, 'Eye of the Storm', *Metropolis*, June 2005, pp.142-9
26 www.idsland.com

Marc Newson

1 Pierre Doze, 'Marc Newson: first the chaise longue, next the cosmos', *Intramuros*, 94, April-May 2001, pp.44-9/102, translation by Sheila O'Leary
2 Simon Mills, 'Watch this space', *Sunday Times Magazine*, 27 November 1994, pp.60-5
3 Alice Rawsthorn, 'An Australian in Paris', *Blueprint*, 104, February 1994, pp.28-31; Caroline Roux, 'Life's a Beach', *Blueprint*, 120, September 1995, pp.11-14
4 Pierre Doze, op. cit.

4   Material Experiments

1 Exhibition gallery text from 'Gaetano Pesce: Il Rumore del Tempo'. Triennale, Milan, 22 January-18 April 2005
2 In April 2005 British retailer Argos was offering a green patio set consisting of four garden chairs and a table made of 'UV stabilised all weather resin' for £29.99. Source: www.argos.co.uk.
3 *The International Design Yearbook*, 1989-90, p.42
4 For example, Starck designed Louis Ghost (2002) and Victoria Ghost (2005) for Kartell; Christophe Pillet's Deauville Armchair for Driade (2005) owes much to Starck's Louis Ghost.
5 Kartell press release, Milan Furniture Fair, 2005
6 See also Gareth Williams, 'Air Chair 1997-1999', in Thimo te Duits (ed.), *The Origin of Things: sketches, models, prototypes*, 2003, pp.234-41, for a fuller discussion of this design.
7 For a more comprehensive examination of work by Bär and Knell and Jane Atfield see Gareth Williams, 'Creating Lasting Values', in Paul Greenhalgh (ed.), *The Persistence of Craft*, 2002, pp.61-72
8 Pot and White collaborated as the Monkey Boys between 1999 and 2003, during which time they made ten

Shrunken benches. Bertjan Pot alone made 20 Shrunken stools and the Dutch firm Goods made a further 100 stools, but Pot was dissatisfied by the quality and they were not a commercial success. Email correspondence between the author and Bertjan Pot, 25 April 2005.

9   Marco Meneguzzo (ed.), *Philippe Starck Distordre: Conversation about design between Alberto Alessi and Philippe Starck*, 1996, pp.43-4

10   Marc Newson: Black Hole table (1988), Mystery clock (1989). Ron Arad: Carbo Tom chair (1997), Carbon-fibre daybed (1998), Carbon Little Heavy chair (2001), Bad Tempered Chair (2002), Carbon Fibre Big Easy chair (2002).

11   Interview with Pol Quadens, in *A+ Architecture, Urbanisme, Design, Arts Plastiques*, 137, December-January, 1995-6, pp.60-3

12   The Spun Carbon chaise longue was exhibited in 'Somewhere Totally Else: The European Design Show', Design Museum, London, 27 September 2003-4 January 2004; Phillips de Pury & Company, New York, 14 December 2004, lot 245; 'Mathias Bengtsson', Röhsska Museet, Göteborg, Sweden, 19 March-8 May 2005

13   Bertjan Pot made two Carbon Copy chairs. One is in the collection of the Boijmans Van Beuningen Museum in Rotterdam (number v 2348) and the other is in the collection of the Stedlijk Museum in Amsterdam.

14   '3 Chairs / 3 Records of the design process', *Interiors*, April 1958, p.119; cited in Pat Kirkham, *Charles and Ray Eames, designers of the twentieth scentury*, 1995, p.240

15   Peter Traag, interview with the author, 24 May 2005

16   *The International Design Yearbook*, 2000, p.63

17   *The International Design Yearbook*, 2000, p.46; *The International Design Yearbook*, 2001, p.43; *iMade*, 2001, pp.114-17; correspondence between Werner Aisslinger and the author, January 2003

18   *iMade*, 2000, p.87

19   Alice Rawsthorn, *Marc Newson*, 1999, p.119. See also Phillips de Pury & Luxembourg, New York, 11 June 2003, lot 214; Christie's, London, 26 May 2005, lot 179.

20   Pamela Buxton, 'Looming Large', *Blueprint*, 169, February 2000, pp.24-6

21   *iMade*, 2001, pp.66-9

22   *iMade*, 2000, pp.38-9. *iMade* 2001, pp.90-93. The Laleggera chair won the Compasso D'Oro award in 1998.

23   *The International Design Yearbook*, 2002, p.141

24   Nick Barley et al, *Lost and Found: critical voices in new British design*, p.80

25   Icon, 23, May 2005, p.69

26   For a fuller examination of the impact of CAD-CAM and rapid prototyping on design and manufacture, see Jane Pavitt, 'Designing in the Digital Age', in Charles Jencks and Maggie Toy (eds.), *Millennium Architecture*, 1999, pp.96-9.

27   www.materialise-mgx.com. Pierre Doze, 'Révolution "Solid"', *Intramuros*, 115, November/December 2004, pp.34-5 (translation by Heidi Ellison, p.90)

Ron Arad

1   *Ron Arad talks to Matthew Collings*, pp.202-4

Gaetano Pesce

1   Gaetano Pesce, interviewed by Justin McGuirk, *Icon*, 15, September 2004

2   Ibid.

5   Design Manifestos

1   Ed van Hinte, *Richard Hutten*, 2002, p.7

2   Ibid.

3   Starck begs to differ, and explains that:
The gold of the weapons represents the collusion between money and war
Table Gun symbolises the East
Bed Side Gun symbolises Europe
Lounge Gun stands for the West
The black shade signifies death
The crosses on the inside are to remind us of our dead ones.
Source: www.philippe-starck.com

4   Jura Koncius, 'A shot in the armchair', *Washington Post*,16 April 2005, p.C01

5   Dunne & Raby, 'Transarchitectures 03' exhibition catalogue, 1998

6   The British Council commissioned Tord Boontje to design the 'Come Rain Come Shine' chandelier for the display 'Brazil 40 Degrees' at Selfridges, London, May 2004. Boontje worked with the Coopa Roca co-operative in Brazil to make the prototype (Phillips de Pury & Company, New York, 8 December 2005, lot.222). Coopa Roca manufacture

smaller production versions, marketed by Artecnica.

7   For further discussion of the Cabinets of Culture see Gareth Williams, 'Creating Lasting Values', in Paul Greenhalgh (ed.) *The Persistence of Craft*, 2002, p.70

8   Email correspondence with Michael Sodeau, 7 June 2005; telephone conversation with Jon Powell, Managing Director of Illizi Home, 16 June 2005

9   Ed van Hinte (ed.), *Eternally Yours: visions on product endurance*, 1997; Ed van Hinte (ed.), *Eternally Yours: Time in Design. Product Value Sustenance*, 2004

10   Anne Marchand, 'Sustainable Users and the World of Objects. Design and Consumerism', in *Eternally Yours*, 2004, p.118

11   Gijs Bakker and Renny Ramakers (eds.), *Couleur Locale*, 1999, p.33. Renny Ramakers (ed.) *Simply Droog*, 2004, p.42-3. Louise Schouwenberg, 'Jurgen Bey', in Ed Annink and Ineke Schwartz (eds.), *Bright Minds, Beautiful Ideas*, Amsterdam, 2003, pp.173-5

12   Gaetano Pesce, exhibition text from 'Gaetano Pesce: Il Rumore del Tempo' exhibition, Triennale, Milan, 22 January-18 April 2005

13   Renny Ramakers and Gijs Bakker (eds.) *Droog Design: Spirit of the nineties*, 1998, p.46

14   Front comprises Sofia Lagerkvist, Charlotte von der Lancken, Anna Lindren and Katja Sövström. They showed in Salonsatellite at the Milan Furniture Fair, April 2004 and their work was included in 'Beauty and the Beast: New Swedish Design', The Crafts Council, London, 18 November 2004-6 February 2005, and 'Designed in Sweden', The Museum of London. See also Anneke Bokern, 'Game of Chance', *Frame*, 45, July-August 2005, pp.60-69; profile by Kieren Long, *Icon*, 27, September 2005, pp.70-6

15   Joanna van der Zanden, *Do Create* brochure, no date (c. 2000)

16   Ibid.

17   See also *The International Design Yearbook*, 2001, pp.84-5

18   Héctor Serrano and Lola Llorca, 'Manolo's gonna have fun', exhibition brochure, 2001

19   Gareth Williams, preface to *Matali Crasset*, 2003, pp.5-11

20   Volker Albus, *The Bookworm by Ron Arad*, 1997; Deyan Sudjic, *Ron Arad*, 1999, pp.103-5

Droog Design

1 Aaron Betsky, *False Flat: Why Dutch Design Is So Good*, 2004, p.172

Dunne & Raby

1 Fiona Raby quoted in Rick Poyner, 'Movers and Shakers', *Financial Times Weekend Magazine*, 19 May 2001, pp.20-2, 40
2 Anthony Dunne and Fiona Raby, *Design Noir: The Secret Life of Electronic Objects*, 2001, charts the 'adoption' of the Placebo objects by members of the public who lived with each of them for a month.

6 Furniture and Lifestyle

1 Andrée Putman, *The International Design Yearbook*, 1992, p.6
2 The Austrian psychologist Alfred Adler (1870-1937) was the first to use the term 'lifestyle' to denote how a person's basic character, established early in childhood, governs his or her reactions and behaviour in later life. Later, writers including George Orwell (1903-1950) and Marshall Macluhan (1911-1980) expanded the definition to be a more general 'way or style of living', with an increasing connotation of life governed by the dictates of the mass media and consumption (OED). Today, arguably, 'lifestyle' is used to mean 'stylish life' and does not refer to ALL styles of living, but to the consumption of the 'things with attitude', referred to in the Introduction.
3 *Elle Decoration*, 1, Summer 1989
4 *I-D*, no.219, April 2002
5 Simon Mills, 'Watch this space', *Sunday Times Magazine*, 27 November 1994, pp.60-5; photographs by Christopher Griffith
6 Marc Newson quoted in Pierre Doze, 'Marc Newson: first the chaise longue, next the cosmos', *Intramuros*, 94, April-May 2001, pp.44-9 (translation by Sheila O'Leary p.102); Samsonite advertisement, *Elle Decoration*, November 2005
7 Mexx advertisement, *Evening Standard ES Magazine*, 27 August 1999
8 *Abitare*, 344, October 1995, p.205
9 Designers in the 1960s and 1970s, such as Mary Quant and Barbara Hulanicki at Biba, made forays into home furnishings too, but Lauren's initiative in the 1980s

10 *The International Design Yearbook*, 2003, p.131
11 *Frame*, 43, March/April 2005, pp.106-7
12 *Orange*, CD by Marcel Wanders and Ton Driessens for Droog Design, included with *Couleur Locale*, *Droog Design for Oranienbaum*, 1999; *Imaginary Discoteca*, CD compiled by Olivier Rohrbach for David Design, Tricatel, 2001; *Cap One*, compiled by Nuphonic Records in co-operation with Cappellini, 2002
13 Moooi catalogue, 2002, p.51
14 Duncan Riches, 'On the Safe Side', *Blueprint*, 230, May 2005, p.122
15 Virginia Postrel, *The Substance of Style*, 2003
16 Jane Lamacraft, 'Keeping up with the Svensons', *Blueprint*, 43, December-January 1988, p.6
17 James Mclean, 'Ikea to set up stores in the high streets', *Evening Standard*, 17 June 2005, p.7
18 'Domus Forum: concerning production design', *Domus*, 759, April 1994, pp.119-22
19 Oliver Finegold and Chris Millar, 'Riot as new Ikea opens', *Evening Standard*, 10 February 2005, pp.10-11
20 Grant Gibson, 'Design for strife', *Guardian*, G2, 23 August 2005, p.7
21 Chris Blackhurst, 'So much more than just a flatpack', *Evening Standard*, 11 February 2005, p.13
22 Peter Kelly, 'Meatballs over Moscow', *Blueprint*, 230, May 2005, p.36
23 Jill Todd, 'Sexy, cool or plain boring?', *Sofastyle*, 28 March-5 April 1998, pp.26-7
24 DFS television advertisement, 2005, PWLC
25 *Evening Standard*, 17 June 2005, p.7, op. cit.
26 Lifestore press and publicity material, February 2004
27 Caroline Roux, 'Life and death at M&S', *Guardian*, Arts, 14 July 2004, p.10
28 Interview with the author, 4 October 2005
29 See Postrel, p.58, for a description of the effect of internet shopping for design items on retailers in the US.
30 Conversation between the author and Alexander Payne, 31 June 2005
31 Annabel Fallon and Sophie Coke-Steel, 'Castors fall off the antiques bandwagon', *Independent on Sunday*, 25 July 2004, p.10
32 *Ron Arad, a retrospective exhibition 1981-2004*, Barry Friedman Ltd, New York, 5 May-24 June 2005; *Ron Arad, new works & installations*, Phillips de

Pury & Company, New York, 2 May-10 June 2005; catalogue published by Barry Friedman Ltd, 2005
33 Interview with Dennis Freedman by Cator Sparks, *Fantastic Man*, 1, Spring & Summer 2005, pp.76-82

Murray Moss

1 Murray Moss interviewed by Gilda Bojardi, *Interni*, 553, July-August 2005, pp.52-9, English translation pp.116-17
2 Linda Hales, 'Glass with Class: For Design Merchant Murray Moss the Future is Clear', *Washington Post*, 19 August 2003, p.C01
3 Interview with the author, 4 October 2005

Ilse Crawford

1 Ilse Crawford quoted by Fiona Rattray, 'Woman of Influence', *Observer Magazine*, 3 July 2005, pp.50-4
2 Interview with the author, 10 August 2005
3 Marianne Macdonald, 'Ilse's interior life', *Evening Standard ES Magazine*, 24 June 2005
4 Interview with the author, op. cit.

Index

Acknowledgements

This book was made possible by the generosity
of the numerous designers and manufacturers
who have freely answered my questions,
explained their work and supplied me with
images. Knowing such interesting people
is the chief reward of such a project. Great
thanks are also due to the specialists, writers,
retailers, exhibition organisers, auctioneers
and gallerists who have assisted with information, shared their views and helped me to form
my ideas. There are too many people to name
individually, but I am grateful to them all.
The V&A Research Department gave me
space to begin writing, and my colleagues
in the Department of Furniture, Textiles and
Fashion have patiently indulged my preoccu-
pation with this project. I am most grateful
to them for giving me time to work on it.
I am particularly indebted to Christopher
Breward, Jane Pavitt and Sorrel Hershberg
whose close attention to the drafts greatly
improved the book. Mike Kitcatt took all
the new photographs of furniture in the
V&A collection that greatly enhance the book.
Mary Butler, Frances Ambler, Clare Davis
and Claire Sawford managed the project
for V&A Publications, Scott Williams and
Henrik Kubel designed a beautiful book.
Finally, I thank Richard Sorger for his
patience, enthusiasm, inspiration and support,
without which this would not have been
written.